CREED OF OUR HOPE

CREED OF
OUR HOPE

by Merrill R. Abbey

ABINGDON PRESS
New York • *Nashville*

CREED OF OUR HOPE

Copyright MCMLIV by Pierce & Washabaugh

Library of Congress Catalog Card Number: 54-10202

Scripture quotations unless otherwise noted are from the Revised Standard Version of the Bible and are copyright 1946
and 1952 by the Division of Christian Education of the
National Council of the Churches of Christ in the U.S.A.

SET UP, PRINTED, AND BOUND BY THE
PARTHENON PRESS, AT NASHVILLE,
TENNESSEE, UNITED STATES OF AMERICA

to LUCY
Partner in Labor
and in Faith

FOREWORD

When my son and I set out for days of canoe camping where the going is rough and portages frequent, we seek to pack in our gear the essentials for comfortable living on the trail, and to eliminate the nonessential. A great creed does that for the mind. It puts minimum essentials in portable form. It becomes a pack-device for carrying basic convictions.

Some of my friends tell me the Apostles' Creed is outdated. I have found it, on the contrary, a flexible symbol of a growing, creative faith. It commends itself to us on several scores. It is short and easily remembered. It speaks in no dry academic terms, but in the pliant picture language that touches the mainsprings of motive. As the most universal of the creeds —used in all branches of Christendom—it has special value for those who strive to build up the spiritual fellowship of the world Church.

These chapters interpret this spiritual classic in the light of experience, cumulative and current, in ministering to students and faculty people in a great state university, as well as to men and women in the swirling tide of civic and industrial life. Here then is a working faith, tested under pressure of the needs of modern minds and affairs.

A Hollywood conversation reported by a columnist reflects a common mood. As the talk of two actresses turned to horoscopes, one remarked, "I didn't know you believed in astrology." "Oh, yes!" her companion replied. "I believe in everything a little bit!" Many a man believes in everything a little bit—in good homes and easy sex standards, democracy and censorship, economic security and inflationary demands, world peace and an armaments race, a Christian society and moral relativity, the Christian faith and the assumption that "all religions come out at the same place in the end." We need to believe in a few central things with clear minds and devoted loyalty.

But there are perplexing questions to be faced. What is dependably real? Is there any authority that can direct our lives? If there is, how can we be true to it without surrendering our birthright of freedom? Can intelligent people of our day believe in spiritual reality that outlives death? Is it possible for God to come into our lives not only as belief but also as direct experience? These and similar questions that trouble many thoughtful people are confronted here. Answers are offered with the hope that they may become useful tools in your own thinking. So used, they can change your life through the buoyancy of a confident and tested hope.

MERRILL R. ABBEY

CONTENTS

1. When Christendom Says, "I Believe"

I believe in . . .

Lynn Harold Hough once gave unforgettable expression to the creative power by which faith becomes the rock foundation of all virile hope. He pointed out:

The great believers are the great adventurers. It is only on a basis of deep assurance regarding central matters that really glorious adventure becomes possible. The chaotic changes which come to the mind which has no indubitable beliefs are a series of nightmares. You need a chart and a compass and a polar star if you are going to sail all about the seven seas. Adventure is only saved from anarchy by great beliefs. Change only becomes evolution when great beliefs lie behind it.

The great believers are the great builders. When life is a whirlwind of wild change you construct tents, but you do not erect great buildings. You must have the assurance of permanence which comes from profound beliefs in order to inspire the confidence which will lead the builders to do their work. You must have great believers if great libraries are to be built. You must have great believers if great cathedrals are to be erected. You must have great believers to inspire the construction of any sort of sound economic and social structure.[1]

[1]Reprinted by permission of *The Pulpit* from the issue of January, 1936, and by permission of the author.

Today, however, thoughtful religious men stand in a strange quandary. On the one hand, they know their inadequacy in themselves to meet the gigantic problems and pressures of this time, so that they must needs fall back on some stored wisdom beyond themselves. But, on the other hand, they know equally that they must not rely on old stereotypes as the answers to new questions. To be adrift in the vast wilderness of the modern world without clear spiritual direction is to risk intolerable lostness, but to be bound by the dead hand of the creeds of yesterday is to be unduly rigid in meeting the emerging problems of a swift-paced time.

In his book *The Great Enterprise* Harry Overstreet sharpens this dilemma. Prime hazard of life in our stage of history's development, he declares, is the unyielding totalitarian mind. Whether we are tyrannized by a government or an ideology, the danger is that of people who must fit new problems into ready-made answers rather than adapt thinking to startlingly new situations and evolve answers that fit the new need. Articles of religious faith, Professor Overstreet suggests, are among these unyielding patterns of thought, mental molds that leave men unfit to face new problems and improvise new answers.

Seeing this hazard in all its peril, a thoughtful man sees also how the most creative improvising is done within some framework of basic belief. Thinking must have a baseline. The sciences, for all their fresh approach to new problems, begin with some undeviating assumptions about the dependability of nature and the discoverability of truth, and their improvising is always within the framework of their basic beliefs.

The improvising that has produced the treasures of Western civilization has occurred within a framework of Christian belief, as Ernest Fremont Tittle reminded us when he wrote:

How wonderful the Christian gospel seemed to the ancient world we moderns can hardly know. In order to know we should have to strip ourselves completely of the things we owe to Christ. Pull down every church and chapel; obliterate the art of Botticelli and the music of Bach; stop the work of the Quakers and every other relief work; wipe out the very idea of voluntary service to others without distinction of nationality, race, color, or class; wipe out all knowledge of a compassion that embraces both friend and foe, and all of faith and hope that has come through Christ; then, if such a thing were possible, you might have some idea of the impression which Christianity made on that ancient pagan world.[2]

More striking still, you might have some idea of how creative life has been within the seemingly fixed framework of a great historic faith!

Repeatedly and forcefully, Jesus underscored this insight. On one memorable occasion a distinguished leader of a community he visited came seeking the healing of his servant and giving evidence of implicit faith in the Master's healing power. Seeing the intensity of the man's faith, Jesus said, "Go; be it done for you as you have believed" (Matt. 7:13). As if to emphasize the point, he said to one whose daughter hovered at the brink of death, "Do not fear, only believe" (Mark 5:36). To another, whose faith that the Master could heal his son took the questioning

[2] *The Gospel According to Luke.* Used by permission of Harper & Bros., publishers.

13

form of the cry, "If you can do anything, have pity on us and help us," Jesus answered, "If you can! All things are possible to him who believes" (Mark 9:22-23). To other sufferers he gave the assurance, "Your faith has made you well" (Matt. 9:22). Such expressions speak of the intensity and power of belief, but they would be meaningless if they did not refer also to its content. Their faith was creative not only because they believed *something* with all their might, but because of *what it was* they believed.

In a conflict of massive ideologies only the great believers have the instruments needed for the central struggle. Machines that grind out an endless flow of goods are not an adequate answer to communist ideas unless the men who handle the machines have a better grasp of life's meaning and purpose, and a deeper understanding of what the good things of life are for, than the communists possess. Bombs that have reached the power of absolute and final destruction can hold no real answer to communist ideas. Only men who deeply hold a truer understanding of where life came from and where it is going, of what it is about and why we have it, can answer the terror-laden ideologies that stalk the earth today. A man who merely improvises his answers to life's deepest questions is no match for a man who has a thought-out answer he deeply believes. And Christians who suppose they can meet communist ideologies by the mere force of their good intentions are doomed to bitter and crushing disillusion.

In this context the major creeds of Christendom are still vitally important. They do not answer life's new questions in detail, but they do give a baseline and a framework for thought. They communicate a vital sense of life's deep and final meaning. A great creed, clearly understood, devotedly pondered, faithfully lived by, need not cripple a man's ability to meet new problems with a free mind. It does give him the chart and compass he needs for any mental voyaging that arrives at a port worth reaching. Approached from this point of view, such a vital statement of historic faith as the Apostles' Creed, in which the major branches of Christendom unite in affirming their faith, can be of inestimable working value. It does not spell out the new answers that must be made to urgent emerging questions, but it does point a direction. Pondering the creed, one can hear the echo of Jesus' voice—"Go; be it done for you as you have believed"—and in this assurance, buttress hope.

I

See how the Apostles' Creed comes to us not only as a pattern of thought handed down through the turns and tests of history, but also as the expression of experience continually fresh and new. One never understands the mighty faith which brought the New Testament into being unless he comes to it as the expression of a powerful creative experience. Not philosophers in their armchairs, but rugged fishermen, carpenters, tentmakers—intrepid adventurers all— stand back of the New Testament. Meeting the man Jesus, they had also met something so utterly changing that nothing in their lives could ever be the same again. This tremendous experience took form in a great commission they remembered from their Master —"Go therefore and make disciples of all nations, baptizing them in the name of the Father and of the Son and of the Holy Spirit" (Matt. 28:19).

Here was a central affirmation, not only of their task but also of their belief. The one great God, in whom as good Jews they had long believed, had come into their lives through a threefold pattern of experience. He was the central principle and power and intelligence back of all creation—God the Father. He was the central reality that made Jesus so creatively, savingly different from all other men—God the Son. He was in the divine unexpectedness of life, the surprising turns of events, the mighty whisperings of conscience, the infinite nearness of a great Companion in prayer—God the Holy Spirit. So this commission became a formula for the baptism of Christian converts and the framework for their instruction. Out of a mighty experience had come this earliest Christian creed: "Go therefore and make disciples of all nations, baptizing them in the name of the Father and of the Son and of the Holy Spirit."

Very early in the growth of Christianity worshipers began to use this simple statement in slightly altered form as an expression of their devotion. In high moments of worship they would say together, "I believe in God the Father Almighty and in Christ Jesus his Son, our Lord, and in holy Spirit, holy Church and resurrection of the flesh." By the middle of the second century this affirmation had gathered about it references to other aspects of Christian life and belief that were vitally meaningful to the Christian community, so that they said together, "I believe in God the Father Almighty; and in Christ Jesus, His only begotten Son, our Lord, who was born of the

16

Holy Spirit and the Virgin Mary, crucified under Pontius Pilate and buried; the third day He rose from the dead, ascended into the heavens, being seated at the right hand of the Father, whence He shall come to judge the living and the dead; and in the Holy Spirit, holy church, forgiveness of sins, resurrection of the flesh." Reshaped to fit the growing experience of Christendom, the creed did not reach its present form until the sixteenth century.

Growing out of experience, it is still mightily relevant to the most crucial experiences of contemporary men. For the modern man needs a basic belief about the nature of the world he lives in—Is it simply material?—and the affirmation, "I believe in God the Father Almighty, Maker of heaven and earth," is not only a statement about God but also about the world itself: it is the kind of world a great God would make and remains dependent upon him.

The modern man needs to have some central authority to which to refer crucial questions of his behavior; and the affirmation, "I believe . . . in Jesus Christ his only Son our Lord," is not only a statement about Christ but also about the final seat of command for our living. The modern man needs some dependable personal resources to live by; and the affirmation, "I believe in the Holy Spirit," is not theology only, but the deepest kind of psychology, assuring us that we live from the ever-flowing springs of life's ultimate reality.

When the modern man says, "I believe . . . in the forgiveness of sins," he is asserting that the last word in personal relationships, whether with God or with other men, is not revenge but a new beginning. When he says, "I believe . . . in the holy catholic Church," he is making an assertion about the inclusiveness of Christian fellowship. When he declares, "I believe . . . in the resurrection of the body and the life everlasting," he speaks a word of confidence that man is not the victim of fate and final extinction, but the inheritor of an invincible destiny and an inalienable dignity.

I never travel in hill country without remembering the psalmist's exclamation, "I lift up my eyes to the hills. From whence does my help come? My help comes from the Lord, who made heaven and earth" (Ps. 121:1-2). Sometimes in weary, hard-pressed moments I shut my eyes and imagine the hills, and in them and these ancient words find rest and assurance. Like everlasting hills are the articles of this ancient creed, which speaks out of experience to experience. Again and again, day after day, I repeat it mentally in my morning devotions; and it lifts my eyes beyond the narrow horizons of my limited life and failing resources and gives me a sense of life's meaning and purpose, its destiny and power. Ancient in its pattern, it is as new as the dawn in the experiences it unlocks. Repeating it, I seem to hear Jesus again—"Go; be it done for you as you have believed."

II

See the Apostles' Creed, again, not only as an expression of central certainties, but also as a symbol of impenetrable mysteries. Since the time of Paul, Christians have been aware that the realities of which their faith speaks are invisible and utterly beyond them, so that only symbols can express them. So Paul himself said, "We look not to the things that are seen but to the things that are unseen; for the things that are seen are transient, but the things that are unseen are eternal." (I Cor. 4:18.)

The language of religion must always be the language of symbol. No one supposes that God's Holy Spirit looks like a dove, yet Christian art so presents it, knowing that it is presenting a mere symbol of what no eye can see. No one supposes that the three interlocking circles often used to represent the Father, Son, and Holy Spirit are an adequate diagram of the relationships within the life of God. Here, rather, is a symbol to suggest "what no eye has seen, nor ear heard." Even the words of our creeds are only symbols to suggest realities that lie beyond our finite minds. From earliest Christian generations the Apostles' Creed itself has been spoken of as a symbol—"Old Roman Symbol" is one of the classic names for it—and as a symbol we must continue to hold it.

While the fullness of the realities of which faith speaks lies beyond our grasp, there are vital certainties we can live by. Like the learned scientist recognizing that his discoveries are but a few pebbles gathered by a child along the shore of the vast ocean of truth, the Christian must in all humility know that his experience of God is but a fragment of the inexhaustible truth. Yet the scientist's knowledge, admittedly incomplete, is nonetheless valid. And the Christian's faith, fragmentary as it is beside the infinite wonder of God, gives him certainties by which he can live with confidence. He knows that final reality is not matter, but Spirit. He knows that the deepest nature of reality is not contradictory to the character revealed in Jesus. Through the creed he gathers up his truest insights into portable form for convenient packing in his mind and into teachable form as a convenient coinage of thought to pass on to succeeding generations.

Living by his certainties, the Christian must be aware of surrounding mysteries. It is no mere naïve anthropomorphism which inspires the moving story in Exodus in which Moses asks to see God's glory. In response, he learns much of God; but he learns, too, that God has great reserve. "Behold," the Lord said, "there is a place by me where you shall stand upon the rock; and while my glory passes by I will put you in a cleft of the rock, and I will cover you with my hand until I have passed by; then I will take away my hand, and you shall see my back; but my face shall not be seen." (33:21-23.) Beyond all primitive pictorial phrasing, here is a profound insight—while we know much of God, we do not know all; we cannot look him level in the eye. We hold up our little cup of experience and understanding, and he fills it to overflowing. Yet the vast sea of his reality cannot be contained in the little cups of our creeds and theologies.

When we lose our grasp of this truth we fall into idolatry. Our creeds become our gods, and we worship the symbol rather than the truth it represents. With the coming of this idolatry we are betrayed into arrogance. We exalt our own interpretations into absolutes and cut off our fellowship with those who understand the symbol in some different way. Only those who bow humbly in the presence of mysteries that fill them with awe have found the truly saving experience of great religion.

III

See the Apostles' Creed, finally, as not only an expression of conviction but also as a salute to the age-old, globe-circling Christian fellowship. It is important for a man to be able to say, "I believe," and mean it. It is vital for a man to hold great convictions so dearly that he will stand by them at all costs. In an age of materialism there is a premium on men who believe that final reality is spiritual. In an age of human enslavement it is vital that a man believe in the dignity of the human person. In an age when the ideas of a "master race" and of "white supremacy" are creating hell on earth, it is of inestimable importance that a man believe that all men are children of God. In the age of the "big lie" there is no hope for us unless we rediscover the power of a truth that does not need to be defended and cannot be warped to fit our private purposes but is itself the mightiest thing in all the world. In an age of consuming anxiety we must for our salvation believe in the final power of goodness and of God.

When men use a historic creed, affirming convictions stanchly held, their act has telling importance not only in stating their beliefs, but also in acknowledging their common allegiance to one Lord, in whose kingdom they participate together. Through the Apostles' Creed not only Protestant but also Roman Catholic and Eastern Orthodox Christians express their faith. Obviously, they are not in full agreement in the details of their theologies. Yet they declare their faith through the symbolism of the same words. Whoever uses this ancient creed thoughtfully, then, must know that it speaks not only his personal con-

21

viction but also his sharing in the most inclusive Christian fellowship.

Using the creed, we do not quibble over details. When a patriot salutes the flag, he does not give blanket approval to every act of his country. He reserves the right to differ with an administration. He remembers that even Lincoln called the Mexican War infamous. Yet he does not withhold the salute to the flag because there are points on which he differs with the policies of government. With deep emotion he makes his salute as an expression of his devotion to the noble heritage his country stands for. Just so the thoughtful Christian does not draw back from use of the creed because there are words or phrases he holds in question. Grateful for the mighty stream of truth and experience out of which it comes, he recites it as an expression of his devotion to the Christian fellowship and to the God who gave it birth and guidance through the maze of the centuries.

As he does so, he can almost hear Jesus saying again, "Go; be it done for you as you have believed," and he moves forward with strength and hope.

2. Where Can Reality Be Found?

. . . God the Father Almighty,
Maker of heaven and earth . . .

In our half-facetious colloquialism, "You can't take it with you," our common speech recognizes that some things apparently real are not at all final. They seem solid enough, but they pass. A man depends on them, but they let him down. Recognizing this inescapable truth, one is forced to ask a straight question: What is real enough to last when all else passes? Where is there a reality that does not fade out somewhere but goes with a man all the way?

As soon as humanity had achieved the ability to think seriously at all, men began to ask this question. The answers have swept a wide circle of variety. One theory in ancient Greece had it that final reality was fourfold—earth, air, fire, and water—and all else depended on these basic elements. Since that day, men who thought the final reality was material have expressed it in various ways. Final reality, said one, is constituted of monads—hard, infinitely minute pellets of the fundamental stuff of the world; in this his theory was not unlike that of today's materialist, who supposes that when you have passed beyond visible substances to molecules, and beyond them to atoms, and beyond them to electrons and protons, you have reached the final reality.

Others there have been who said, This preoccupation with material stuff misses reality altogether. The basic content of reality is rather in the idea. An ideal pattern, a kind of disembodied blueprint, is the one abiding truth, to which all else owes its existence. The hard stuff of life can be destroyed, but not the idea. It has the only independent being; and as long as it is there, all else is possible.

To this considerable group of thinkers still others have made answer: Even a reality so intangible as the disembodied idea cannot be fully credited. The only thing that endures is change. Even while you are observing and analyzing it, your supposed reality has moved on in the ceaseless flow of change; and this never-ending flux alone is real.

Ah, sighs another group, even a reality composed only of change is impossible; for there is nothing real. The whole vast cosmic show is mere illusion, and your quest leads in the end to Maya, universal mirage. Where can reality be found? Nowhere. For there is none.

If such speculations strike you as hopelessly academic mental gymnastics, leading nowhere, see where the quest comes out in the modern world. Karl Marx built his system of thought and life on his own estimate of reality. The only realities that count, he said, are the economic ones. Man is not a creature of soul or spirit, but only of body: an economic animal whose motives are limited to his bread-and-butter desires. Beyond these nothing is real—unless it be the final forces of history, self-operating automatic movements from thesis to antithesis and back to synthesis, one state of affairs flowing irresistibly from another in spite of the supposed choices and purposes of men. This conception of reality, embodied in the Communist Revolution, has made a difference far from academic.

As the Communist Revolution rested on one view of reality, the American Revolution stood on another. For the founders of this republic had a profound reading of man's meaning as more than economic producer and consumer. They believed in human dignity, holding it self-evident "that all men are created equal; that they are endowed by their Creator with certain unalienable rights." The final reality, then, is not matter, but spirit; man is a child of God and has his dignity in consequence of this fact. The final force in the world is truth, which can be trusted to defend and vindicate itself so long as there is a free interplay of ideas in an open forum where error need not be feared when truth is not bound. This, too, is a reading of reality; and its consequences have been far from academic.

Christianity has its own reading of reality, which in the classic words of the Apostles' Creed is this: "I believe in God the Father Almighty, Maker of heaven and earth." Back of all else, Christianity holds, stands this final truth. On it all else rests. From it life derives its meaning. Amid the clash of systems based on the clash of estimates of the real, this Christian answer is so crucially important that I ask you to look at it carefully with me.

I

Competent and penetrating minds throughout the centuries have found ample reasons to believe this was the true reading of reality. In the golden age when the classic philosophers swayed the mind of Greece and the greatest prophets forged the conscience of Israel, one poetic thinker cast a sentence which has commanded the respect of all succeeding generations: "In the beginning God created the heavens and the earth" (Gen. 1:1).

Practical men in all ages have felt that it made demands on their credulity which they could not meet to suppose that this vast universal process "just happened." The better they have understood its immensity and the complexity of its structure, the more they have been convinced that a creative mind must have conceived it; until one comes to a modern philosopher of science like Sir James Jeans, testifying that the more we know of the universe the less it resembles a great machine and the more it resembles a great thought. Or one hears a scientific thinker like Du Noüy explaining the overwhelming odds against the evolving of intricately organized life with its own directive intelligence by the mere repetitions of random chance. The universe we know, to such thinkers, is inconceivable unless back of it stands creative Intelligence.

Immanuel Kant was suggesting another reason that has persuaded far-ranging minds of the truth of Christianity's reading of reality when he declared that of all the impressive phenomena of the world only two filled him with deathless wonder—"the starry heavens above and the moral law within." As hard to explain as an intricate visible universe would be without a Creator, it would be no harder than a man's saying, "I ought," and "I must," and doing rigorously demanding duties for no other reason than that he could not escape a stern conscience—unless that conscience relates itself to some reality deeper than the man's own consciousness.

Moses faced this stern inner sense of *ought* and asked its name. What or who was driving him to do the impossible in his struggle for Israel's freedom? "Who shall I say sent me?" And the answer came back, "I am who I am" (Exod. 3:14). In one way or another the truest men have faced such absolutes in their consciences until they have been convinced they were face to face with fundamental reality—with God.

Those who have thought most carefully about the universe that is our home have been most impressed with its unity. Nothing moves independently of all the rest. When a newly discovered planet deviates a hair's breadth from the projected course its known movements have plotted, you can conclude that it is not acting independently; but that other forces, not a part of your original reckonings, are at work so that from the minute deviation you can derive the exact position where a hitherto unknown planet should swim into view. Train your telescope on that sector of the heavens, and there is the planet no human eye has previously seen. Whence comes such unity? Penetrating minds, not a few, conclude there is a pointer to basic reality in such an insight as Augustus Wright Bamberger put into haunting verse:

> There's a part of the sun in the apple,
>   There's a part of the moon in a rose;
> There's a part of the flaming Pleiades
>   In every leaf that grows.

Out of the vast comes nearness;
  For the God whose love we sing
Lends a little of His heaven
  To every living thing.

II

"I believe in God the Father Almighty, Maker of heaven and earth"—if this reading of reality has commended itself to the competent and penetrating mind, it has appealed even more powerfully to the probing and testing experience of those who have lived most fully.

A physiologist may define life as "the recurrent satisfaction and dissatisfaction of a protein molecule" and in so doing cover neatly certain areas of experience opened up in the laboratory of one field of research. Who that has lived with any fullness, however, would suppose that such a definition covered the whole range of experience? A shoreline silhouetted against the sunset of a serene summer evening, and the long, long thoughts it inspires—where do these fall in the limited range of "the recurrent satisfaction and dissatisfaction of a protein molecule"?

A picket frozen on duty—
  A mother starved for her brood—
Socrates drinking the hemlock,
  And Jesus on the rood.[1]

How will you cover these in "the recurrent satisfaction and dissatisfaction of a protein molecule"? Such a working assumption may do very well for certain

[1] "Evolution" by William H. Carruth. Used by permission of Mrs. William H. Carruth.

limited laboratory purposes, but there are ranges of experience such animalism cannot cover.

James Branch Cabell defined life in another way. It is nothing but "a comedy perfectly re-enacted," he said. And sometimes the cycle of our petty foibles lends credence to his judgment, until we understand the boredom of the cynic who wrote Ecclesiastes: "The thing that hath been, it is that which shall be; and that which is done is that which shall be done: and there is no new thing under the sun" (Eccl. 1:9, K.J.V.). This covers much of our experience; but will it cover all? Can you get Othello, and Hamlet, and Lear into the groove of that broken record of triviality? Will it do to describe the profound events of the Garden of Gethsemane and the hill called Calvary in such a way?

In an age like ours the pessimists find a plausibility in events that seems to sustain their estimate of life's meaning. Bertrand Russell speaks to much that we can share with him when he says, "The life of Man is a long march through the night, surrounded by invisible foes, tortured by weariness and pain, towards a goal that few can hope to reach, and where none may tarry long." Out of the travail of postwar Europe, Jean-Paul Sartre speaks a word this generation is keyed to understand:

We are isolated. We are conscious of our isolation. We make foolish and pathetic efforts to escape it. . . . Man can do nothing unless he first understands he must count on no one but himself, that he is alone, abandoned on earth in the midst of his infinite responsibilities, without help, with no other aims than the ones he sets for himself, with no other

destiny than the one he forges for himself on this earth. . . .
Life is absurd, love is impossible. . . . There is no way of
knowing the true meaning of what we are doing; perhaps
our actions have no meaning.[2]

Profoundly as one sympathizes with the plight of
peoples whose bitter lot has pushed them to such
extremities of disillusion, one who has moved about
in postwar Europe is also conscious of great areas of
experience in which hope is vitally alive because effort
is keyed to a deeper reality based on faith's conviction that life's final springs flow ceaselessly from "God
the Father Almighty, Maker of heaven and earth."
Those who in the troubled areas of the human pil-
grimage have most lastingly influenced the course of
events have drawn their strength from this deeper
reading of reality.

So Paul, establishing the westward line of march of
our civilization, declared, "We know that in everything God works for good with those who love him"
(Rom. 8:28) . So Isaiah, in an age of unutterable weariness and despair, asserted, "They who wait for the
Lord shall renew their strength" (Isa. 40:31) . And
centuries later, an explorer like Stanley could set down
his experience that he could march farther, bear
heavier burdens, and be less exhausted at the end of
the day than his nonpraying companions. So Robert
Louis Stevenson, thinking back to a time when his life
changed course for the immeasurably better, could
pronounce that "I came about like a well-handled

[2] This, and the foregoing quotations from Russell, Ecclesiastes,
Cabell, and the unnamed physiologist, are taken from Bosley,
Preaching on Controversial Issues, pp. 55-56.

ship. There stood at the wheel that unknown steersman whom we call God."

Out of profound depths of experience faith draws the grounds for its reading of reality—"I believe in God the Father Almighty, Maker of heaven and earth."

III

In a time like ours, when—particularly for the young, whose affairs seem in the grip of forces vast and impersonal, outside themselves—it is difficult to keep any sense of purpose in life, this reading of reality has an importance beyond all exaggeration. For in the light of such conviction personal living is lifted out of the categories of chance, and purpose finds its champion and guide.

There is a memorable passage in the autobiography of Fred B. Smith, in which this pioneer of the Y.M.C.A. movement describes a meeting with Herbert Spencer. He had gone reluctantly to have tea with Spencer, dreading the possibility of being drawn into an argument with the aged philosopher, whom he looked upon as an unbeliever. Toward the close of the evening Spencer said to him, "I think you are the man who has been speaking to our young men." When Smith admitted that he was, Spencer continued, "When you are speaking to young men throughout the country and the world, say to them for me that the great 'First Cause' had a thought about each of them before they were born." As they took their leave, Spencer added, "The most important thing in every life is to learn what that thought was of the First Cause."

In the coldly unemotional language of the secular

philosopher this is what great religion means when it talks of life as a plan of God. In a day like ours, when military service and war and a host of other factors he would not have chosen beat with their adverse winds against a young man's life, it is still possible to make the major decisions and the daily responses in the light of loyalty to God's plan; and those who live most meaningfully will still be those who live responsive to that "thought of the First Cause."

Nor need the intelligent be confined to abstractions about some remote First Cause. Blaise Pascal's was one of the most scintillating intellects of modern times, amazing the learned world with brilliant contributions to mathematical thought while still in his teens, probing among the phenomena of physics to discover the law of fluid pressures that still bears his name, enriching thought and understanding in many fields. After his death there was found written on a slip of worn paper carried near his heart, the discovery that Pascal believed to have been his greatest: "that God is not the God of philosophy, but that he is the God of Abraham, of Isaac, of Jacob, and of Jesus." So the profound thinker placed at the head of all his learning the truth that God is not abstract principle, but personal reality, whom we can know and who knows us, with whom we can have dealings, who leads us to fuller life, and in communion with whom we can discover life's truest purposes.

There have been those who believed that because life was a plan of God, it was all mapped and foreordained; and what would be, would be. Such belief left men in the hands of a God who shaped their lives by forces outside themselves, over which they could have no control, and to which they could only respond as God directed. Any thoughtful man must see that much concerning life is given, apart from any choice of his. The circumstances of birth, health, and opportunity shape much of a man's course. But do they pronounce the final verdict?

Well, here is a soldier on a hospital bed, both his arms blown away, both his legs amputated, with only a fighting chance to live. What can life hold for him? To a buddy he says, "Do something for me, will you? Reach in that locker and get out the little blue book. Now read me John 3:16, do you mind?" The old words on God's love, which will never fail and is for "whoever believes in him," come with a new warmth and power. The soldier says to himself, "I'm 'whoever'!" He hangs onto the thought. The sense of a love that still has a purpose for him gives him strength. He rallies from shock and begins a convalescence that amazes the surgeon when he stops in his next round.

"What made the change?" the surgeon asks; and the soldier, for reply, directs him, "Reach into that locker and get out the little blue book. Now find John 3:16 and read it to me." Then it occurs to him that his chance to make his life count lies in this simple act. A score of times a day, as visitors, nurses, doctors, comrades stop at his bedside, the soldier repeats his request as if it were a new idea. Each time the familiar words are read, he finds a new opportunity to discuss what this truth means to him. When at last his recovery has gone so far that artificial limbs become possible, he sees these as an open door to a new career, for they will enable him to go about freely and preach the truth that has made the mighty difference to him.

War and wounds had gone far to draw their limiting circle around the soldier's life. They had set the stage, but they could not quite manage to dictate the action. Instead of hopelessness he found a mighty hope; instead of uselessness and despair, a new and thrilling way of usefulness and something newly challenging to live for.

William James, seeing how forces play upon our lives, but cannot quite overcome our power to make an answer of our own, concluded that God is at work with us, as if he were a master chess player matching his wits with our amateur moves. He knows every move that we can make—not in the sense that they are all prescribed before they are made, but as the chess master does, who knows every move that can be made on the board, and is ready with an answering move for each. So, William James suggested, God is at work with us, matching move for move; and no matter how much life circumscribes our seeming opportunities, we and God can work out the answering play together.

How vital that we come to know such a God, living our lives not as unconscious beneficiaries of his goodness, but as conscious co-workers with him, so that by prayer and the disciplines of great religion we find our way to the fullest life, in touch with the most abiding reality. There was a day when, watching a religious processional carrying a crucifix through the streets of Paris, Voltaire, widely known as a brilliant infidel, raised his hat. "What!" exclaimed a friend, "you, acknowledging God?" Laconically Voltaire replied, "We salute, but we do not speak." For how many a man this is true! How immeasurably richer life might be for some of us if now we were to move to a conscious acknowledgment and loyal dependence on the God whose reality we have long dimly known.

3. Thou Seemest Human and Divine

. . . and in Jesus Christ his only Son our Lord;
who was conceived by the Holy Spirit,
born of the Virgin Mary, suffered under Pontius Pilate;
was crucified, dead, and buried . . .

It was Harry Emerson Fosdick who gave currency to the whimsical story of the club where a member named Crowe seized upon every possible occasion to parade his disbelief in the Christian faith, until a snatch of verse appeared on the bulletin board:

> We've heard, in language highly spiced,
> That Crowe does not believe in Christ;
> But what we'd really like to know
> Is whether Christ believes in Crowe!

That gets hold of an important matter by the right end.

For what any one of us thinks of Christ is not vastly important to the world. There was a time when it was seriously debated whether or not he had actually lived. Now it has been established beyond serious doubt as one of the best-attested facts of history, and his character is recognized by historians as better known than any other of the ancient world. No writer can now be taken seriously in the attempt to disprove his having lived; but beyond the mere fact of his existence at a given point in history, he has entered into every aspect of our culture until there is no understanding our literature, music, painting, sculpture, or our basic ideas in human relations and government, apart from him.

Nevertheless, what I think of Christ is important, for it makes a vast difference to me. He presents questions to the mind, so disturbing that we cannot dismiss them and cannot live at peace with our own thoughts until we arrive at some working answer to them. As Harry Kemp said:

I cannot put the Presence by, of Him, the Crucified,
Who moves men's spirits with His Love as doth the moon
    the tide.

. . . .

Still speaking to the hearts of men—though shamed and
    crucified,
The Master of the Centuries who will not be denied! [1]

As the museum guide said to the superficial visitor who dismissed art masterpieces with a wave of the hand—"For some centuries now, the pictures in this gallery have not been judged by the tourists; the tourists have been judged by the pictures"—so the possibility grows on us that what we think of him may well turn out to be a kind of judgment on ourselves. There is even the possibility that our failure to think clearly about him is resulting in some personal loss, as when the world condemned itself to loss of light and power by its idle legends and vague theories about lightning, until Benjamin Franklin with his kite and his key clarified thought and made a personal appropriation.

[1] "The Voice of Christmas." Used by permission of the author.

Basic thinking about Christ has held a central place in the life of Christendom from the dawning days of our faith. One hears it reflected in the amazingly varied liturgies of Protestant, Roman Catholic, and Eastern Orthodox Christians, as their worship shares this common declaration: "I believe in . . . Jesus Christ [God's] only Son our Lord; who was conceived by the Holy Spirit, born of the Virgin Mary, suffered under Pontius Pilate, was crucified, dead, and buried; the third day he rose from the dead; he ascended into heaven, and sitteth at the right hand of God the Father Almighty; from thence he shall come to judge the quick and the dead."

No wise man will dismiss what that creed stands for merely because he disagrees with the connotation of some of its words or phrases. There is the possibility that one has not understood what it is trying to say! Some years ago, when I was pastor of a downtown metropolitan church, my weekly sermon themes were posted on a signboard conspicuously displayed where the city's heaviest traffic passed. One man, whose letters admitted he had never attended the church, used to read the subjects, imagine fantastic things he was sure I said about them, and then write me heated letters pointing out the folly of my ideas! Sometimes, when I hear people rejecting the brawny concepts of Christianity because of some imagined difference about a word, I am reminded of that anonymous correspondent!

How shall we think of Christ? His commanding place in the world's life, utterly beyond dispute, gives force to Richter's characterization—"who, . . . holiest among the mighty, . . . mightiest among the holy, lifted . . . empires off their hinges and turned the stream of centuries out of its channel, and still governs the ages." Entering into the growing experience of discipleship, through the gateway of clearer under-standing of what the Christian centuries have found his life to mean, can bring home to us, one by one, what has been vividly real and inestimably precious to that multitude who have proclaimed him as the world's best hope.

I

Any serious facing of central Christian thinking about Christ brings one, first, to Christendom's basic conviction that his coming was a human event, and his significance is to reveal the possibilities of human nature. Although Christian thought has been con-cerned about the divinity of Christ, it has held tena-ciously to the belief that he was fully and vigorously human. Whatever we believe about his divinity, the greatest theologians and councils of the church have insisted, must be such as not to conflict with this elemental fact of his humanity.

The first great theological battle waged by the Christian church was not to protect the idea of his divinity against claims that he was human, but to defend the fact of his humanity against the notion that he was only divine. So the creed is at pains to as-sert some essential human facts that identify him with us—he was born, suffered, died, was buried. He was no ghostly spiritual figure who slipped into the world through some other gate than birth, was too divine to suffer, or escaped the world through some other exit than death. He was, first of all, intensely human, sharing with us the common human experiences in their most limiting forms.

Probably no phrase in the creed has occasioned more difficulty to thoughtful people in our generation than the statement that he was "born of the Virgin Mary." It is worth noting that beyond a doubt this phrase first appeared in the creed not so much to rivet attention on some special miracle in regard to his birth, as to note the basic historical reality that *he was born*. He is not an abstract idea. He is not a legendary figure. He is not an angelic visitor from some other sphere. He stands in the stream of history as one we can know, "born of the Virgin Mary"; and this phrase simply mentions without debate the identifying name of his mother.

That some miracle of his birth is not the central matter should be apparent to any careful reader of the New Testament, the major bulk of which is made up of the letters of Paul, which are the earliest Christian documents to come down to us. For a period of some twenty years, beginning soon after the events of Jesus' life, Paul was engaged in writing these epistles. He was not only nearest the events in time, but was also deeply concerned with the divinity of Jesus. The loftiest conceptions of Christian theology stem from the writings of Paul. So much so, indeed, that Paul has been accused in some quarters of substituting a divine Saviour for the simple teacher of Galilee. Yet in all his writing, over that vastly influential twenty-year span, Paul only once mentioned the birth of Jesus, and then only in a casual reference to him as "born of woman," with no possible connotation of a special miracle. The very least this can mean is that Paul either held his high conception of a divine Christ without having heard of a virgin birth or, having heard of it, did not hold it basically essential to Christian faith in a divine Saviour.

Not only so, but also of two of the four Gospels the same may be said. Mark was the earliest Gospel to be written, about A.D. 70. It was an attempt to tell the central things about Jesus which Christians needed to know and believe. Yet it has no story of his birth. Rather it begins with him in the full tide of his manhood, entering upon his public ministry. Since Mark's Gospel long circulated independently before it was gathered into a biblical collection with other Gospels, it seems clear that it contained what the writer believed to be the essential facts; so that one is led to conclude either that Mark believed in Christ without knowing of a special miracle concerning his birth, or that, knowing it, he did not consider it essential to Christian faith and knowledge.

Of all the Gospels, John presents the most exalted view of Jesus. These things, the author declares, "are written that you may believe that Jesus is the Christ, the Son of God, and that believing you may have life in his name" (John 20:31). Every strand of material which could be made to serve this purpose is pressed into use in this beloved Gospel. Yet there is no story of the birth of Jesus. In its place stands a philosophical prologue adapting the Greek idea of a divine Logos to the purposes of Christian thought. From this, John

41

plunges directly into the adult life and ministry of Jesus. If John had thought that some circumstance concerning Jesus' birth would help his readers to believe him "the Christ, the Son of God," it is only too clear that he would have used it. That he did not is an indication either that he did not know the theory and yet believed as he did, or that, knowing it, he did not consider it essential to belief that "Jesus is the Christ, the Son of God."

All of this is said neither to prove nor to disprove a miracle of virgin birth, but to recall that from the earliest times there have been among the most devout Christian saints those who, either believing or disbelieving it, held a high allegiance to Christ on other grounds. Before all else Christians have seen Jesus' coming as a human event, and his character as a revelation of what, under God, human nature might be. Multitudes of devout Christians can join in Richard Watson Gilder's declaration:

> If Jesus Christ is a man—
>   And only a man,—I say
> That of all mankind I cleave to him,
>   And to him will I cleave alway.

When we are depressed by our failures and betrayals of our highest ideals, he saves us from despair concerning our human possibilities; for he too is a fact about human nature. Coming out of the loins of the race, he is the pioneer and demonstration of what our humanity can be. He punctures and deflates our flimsy excuse that, human nature being what it is, these sorry performances are all we can rightfully expect of ourselves. He gives substance to the hope that, in all the earthiness of our humanity, we are yet meant for better things.

II

One cannot seriously face Christian thinking about Jesus, however, without seeing, too, that his coming stands forth as a divine event, revealing the nature and character of God. Not that Christians have believed that all of God was contained in the tiny, precious bundle that lay in Mary's arms in the manger of Bethlehem. The throne of the universe was not vacant while Jesus walked the shores of Galilee. When he died upon the cross, God did not cease to exist. It was because God continued, unextinguishable, deathless, invincible, that the grave could not hold Jesus. When, on many occasions, Jesus prayed to his heavenly Father, he obviously believed there was more of God than existed in his own life, and was not merely talking to himself!

Yet he was different from any other who has ever lived. He made a transforming difference in every life he touched. Zacchaeus the tax collector, after a day with him, turned from his graft to a new life of exemplary honesty and generosity. Mary Magdalene, under his influence, turned from unrestrained passion to memorable purity. Peter, living with him, grew from an undependable victim of his own tempestuous impulses to the "Rock" of dependability Jesus had seen in him. John was remolded by him from one given to such vehement outbursts of temper as to win the nickname "Son of Thunder," to the memorable apostle of love. No other teacher has made such a transforming difference, with such far-reaching implications, in the lives of so many of his followers; so that those who came to know Jesus best came to the belief that God touched them through his life and influence.

Nor did these transformations cease when Jesus was no longer physically present. Napoleon, marveling at the effect of Jesus on the life of the world, observed that he, too, could sway vast crowds; but added that his influence depended on the magnetic quality of his presence, while Jesus alone could continue to mold the lives of multitudes long after he was gone. Such influence spans the centuries, transforming Augustine from libertine to saint; washing the pride away from Francis of Assisi, until his humility and love are the fairest achievement of the amazing thirteenth century; drawing the church back from pompous artificiality to the essential simplicities through the change in the life of Martin Luther in the sixteenth century; bringing a new breath of spiritual reality to the jaded life of England through the transformation of John Wesley in the eighteenth century; and in this bloodiest century of human history furnishing the driving motives that make the name of Albert Schweitzer memorable for many-sided achievement, unbelievable self-sacrifice, and glorious human service. No ethical teacher of the ages has had this far-ranging effect on the transforming of countless lives flung across the centuries; until Christians cannot but believe that through Jesus they have an authentic contact with God.

Apart from this belief it is difficult to make sense

of many of Jesus' own words. His personal humility was one of his most striking qualities; yet his demand for personal allegiance was absolute, expressing his belief that in giving allegiance to him his followers gave themselves to more than a man, to the ultimate reality of the universe, to very God. When a disciple asked to be shown the heavenly Father, Jesus replied, "He who has seen me has seen the Father" (John 14:9). He said, "I am the way, and the truth, and the life; no one comes to the Father, but by me." (John 14:6.) He called himself the bread of life, the water of life, the vine of which we are but branches, the resurrection and the life. In view of what he had to say about himself, there are just three possibilities: he was either a deluded victim of his own megalomania, or history's supreme impostor, or what he said he was—a revelation of the nature and character of God.

The effect of utter sincerity which he has had upon the most careful historical students; the way his life hangs together in one piece; the influence he continues to have on multitudes of men across the ages—these things make it impossible to believe he was deluded or a deceiver. Nineteen centuries of the way he has stood up under historical study and remained himself a maker of history verify his sincerity and sanity. There is left but one conclusion. His own estimate of himself was true: through him we best meet God. Multitudes of thoughtful men and women join in the other half of Gilder's declaration:

> If Jesus Christ is a God—
>   And the only God,—I swear

I will follow him through heaven and hell,
The earth, the sea, the air!

III

Serious thinking about Jesus leads to the conviction that his coming was a human event, showing the possibilities of our human nature; a divine event, revealing the nature and character of God; and also an atoning event, presenting a saving reality in the midst of suffering. This is not to plead for acceptance of all the symbolic figures through which men in various periods have attempted to describe or explain the significance of the sufferings of Jesus. It has been suggested that his death was a ransom paid to the devil to secure the release of mankind from bondage to evil; or that God was so bound by his own sense of justice that he could not forgive his children until someone had suffered in due proportion for our sins, and that Jesus presented himself to suffer in our stead and so release us from God's wrath. Such figures of speech may have helped men at some times in some aspects of their thinking, but their limitations are serious.

Paul frees such thinking from its burden of artificiality as he points out that Jesus was not man's sacrifice, to appease the wrath of an angry God, so much as God's self-revelation, that men might see his love and respond to him. So Paul declares, "God was in Christ reconciling the world to himself, not counting their trespasses against them, and entrusting to us the message of reconcilation." (II Cor. 5:19.) Here is the atoning reality of Christ. Through him our estrangement is replaced by at-one-ment. In his one life we

see God's picture of what he meant us to be, and
man's best picture of what God is. In his love we see
the everlasting love of God, which melts our resistance
and wins us to God. If God is like that, men say, he is
my God, and I must everlastingly belong to him. I
must love him with all my heart, and soul, and mind,
and strength.

All this comes to a focus in the suffering of Christ,
which the faith of Christendom cannot forget. By his
suffering he showed the extent of his love. If his
nature is the reflection of the nature of God, we see
through him how much God loves. In his suffering
we see something about our own. We cannot believe
that God made him suffer because he was angry with
him, or that it was God's deepest intention that he
should suffer. God, we believe, wanted only good for
his Son. Yet, given the evil of the world, God's will
under the circumstances was that his Son should
suffer rather than prove unfaithful. And God shared
his suffering with him and saw to it that out of the
suffering came a greater good.

We believe this is a clue to the reality back of our
sufferings. They are not visitations of God's wrath, nor
are they reflections of God's wish that we suffer. He
wants only good for us. Yet, given the circumstances of
the world, it is God's will that his children bear their
suffering with loyalty to all that is best. And he is
with us in it. "In everything God works for good with
those who love him" (Rom. 8:28), and out of the
worst he often brings the best.

Here, then, stands a great and glorious Christ, near
to us in our humanity to lead the way; above us in

his divinity to release powers in us greater than our own, through which we become what we could not be without him; with us even in suffering, to bring from it God's perfect will. No wonder Paul, contemplating all this, exclaimed, "Christ in you, the hope of glory" (Col. 1:27). What a day this would be for you, my friend, if it brought you to him in a new and final allegiance!

4. Resurrection—
A Mighty Challenge

*. . . the third day he rose from the dead;
he ascended into heaven, and sitteth at the right hand of
God the Father Almighty;
from thence he shall come to judge the quick and the dead.*

Datelined Jerusalem, one of the pivotal sentences
of all history reads, "So they went and made the
sepulchre secure by sealing the stone and setting a
guard" (Matt. 27:66). There is no hint of the dawn
that changed the world, no trace of the twilight at
Emmaus when the commonplace caught the glow of
a living presence that drove all discouragements away.
Yet Christianity's march through the world unmistakably starts here, with a grave that cannot be
casually left to the quiet dark.

As if a felon's grave were not secure enough already! The man was dead, wasn't he? A scourge, and
nails, and a Roman javelin had seen to that. Not
only dead, but also discredited—denounced by the
religious leaders, sentenced to death by the government, hooted by the crowd who watched him die.
Polluted sources of information would do the rest,
as the men who were determined that his name and
influence should die with him arranged to have the
story published as best suited them. Just to make
doubly sure, "they went and made the sepulchre
secure by sealing the stone and setting a guard."

If this had been the end of the matter, Christendom's creeds would have concluded with the leaden words "crucified, dead, and buried." Or perhaps it is more accurate to say there would have been no creeds, and no Christendom. For there would have been no living Christ—only another martyred prophet. With a catch in its heart the world might recall his wistful memory, and life would be fairer for the recollection. But there would be no creative faith in a Christ backed by deathless reality, no power to challenge the evils of generations yet to be or to build new civilizations on old ruins.

One sentence in the record, however, changes everything. "Behold, there was a great earthquake; for an angel of the Lord descended from heaven and came and rolled back the stone, and sat upon it." (Matt. 28:2.) In all their calculations the men of power had forgotten to reckon with an earthquake or a living spirit. What can a stone or a military guard do to hold back such forces? This was not the last time elaborate plans have gone awry through such miscalculations. Stones keep having a bad time with earthquakes, and troops have often proved no match for a great soul.

Yet the tomb did look dreadfully secure. Even Jesus' most devoted friends had no doubt about its finality. When the women came to visit the garden, it was only to pay some last reverence to an honored body. Finding the tomb empty, they could think of only one explanation, which Mary expressed between sobs: "They have taken away my Lord, and I do not know where they have laid him" (John 20:13). Later, on the way to Emmaus, two of the disciples walked with Jesus; they were so sure he was dead that it was only at long last they recognized his presence. Thomas put the matter in the sensible way many of us would have liked to do if we had been there: "Unless I see in his hands the print of the nails, and place my finger in the mark of the nails, and place my hand in his side, I will not believe" (John 20:25). They knew a secure tomb when they saw one, and did not leap to easy conclusions of a resurrection from some meager data of an empty grave, or an earthquake, or a vision.

When they did change their minds, it was because they had met another range of facts than these. You do not know a man to be alive because his grave is empty. But if you meet a presence sufficiently verified, this may convince you. And they met a presence. It was so amazing that in their excitement they could not be sure of all the details, so that the stories they told about it have many differences among them, as the testimony of dependable but excited witnesses often does. Yet it convinced them beyond all doubt.

A recent writer imagines a meeting with Simon, James, and John, as they shuffled along a road a few hours after the Crucifixion.

"Why so downhearted, Peter?" you ask.

"Jesus is dead," he answers.

"Well, James, why are you so glum?"

"Jesus is dead."

"John, what has gone wrong with you?"

"Jesus is dead."

Pressing the conversation a little more, you inquire further.

"Well, what are you going to do now, Peter?"

"Go back to my trade, fishing."

"And you, James and John, what will you do?"

"Back to mending nets."

Not much left for these men. They're done in, if men ever were.

Meet them again three days later. Did you ever see such a change? Their feet hardly seem to touch the ground!

"Why so elated, Peter?" you ask.

"Jesus is alive!"

"Why are you so exuberant, James?"

"Jesus is alive!"

"Well, John, what makes you so happy?"

"Jesus is alive!" [1]

The only thing imaginary about this is the form of the conversation. The change is a matter of record. What the change accomplished is the principal turning point in the history of the Western world.

Not these three only, but a great company of the friends of Jesus—sensible people, who knew a secure tomb when they saw one—became equally sure that Jesus was alive. When they went out to preach, this was their message: not merely "Jesus taught," or "Jesus died," but "Jesus is alive!" For two thousand years this has been the Christian message. Twenty centuries of fierce scrutiny, and the message still carries power.

"The third day he rose from the dead." But for

[1] These imaginary conversations are adapted from Lloyd R. Gillmet's contribution to the anthology *Best Sermons* of 1951-52, edited by G. P. Butler. Copyright 1952. Used by permission of The Macmillan Co.

the fact this clause reflects, there could be no creed, for there would be no Christian message. This fact is the fulcrum of history, the focal point of Christianity's reading of reality. But it is more. It is a constant challenge to the pretensions of men. Through it divinity keeps breaking into our humdrum existence with a personal challenge for each of us.

I

For one thing, it challenges the world's accepted authorities. Make no mistake about it, real authority had made the tomb secure. Caiaphas was the high priest of one of the world's greatest religions. Pilate was the provincial governor, with the authority of empire behind him. These authorities had agreed in the condemnation, in the seal on the stone, and in the guard. Learning, religion, and empire were speaking with a common voice; and if anyone dared to question, back of them, as a court of last appeal, stood Caesar. Real authority made the tomb secure; but another voice has the last word. It is Jesus, saying, "All authority in heaven and on earth has been given to me" (Matt. 28:18). Which are you going to believe?

Well, go to Rome. The Forum, the Colosseum, the Circus, the crumbling walls, the ancient roads leading out to the imperial frontier—these are deeply impressive relics of a grandeur that is gone, monuments to a memory. But everything that is vibrantly alive in Rome is related, not to the fallen empire, but to the living Christ. In Paris a few antiquities, like the ruins of the Roman baths, recall an authority, once invincible but now long dead; but the throngs in

Notre Dame, the processionals in Sacre Coeur, the kneeling multitudes in a thousand churches, know the authority of a living Christ. The authority that made the tomb secure reached even to the north of England, so that tramping the roads of the Lake District, you come upon the ruins of Roman outposts; but it is an authority long dead, while at the heart of every village are the marks of the homage living people pay to a living Christ.

Strangely enough, a world of authority continues to dismiss him and make his tomb secure. During Lent, 1953, an editorial writer described the current atomic bomb test in the Nevada desert as if it were a massive service of worship. The devotees knelt in their trenches before the great god of power, as in a blinding flash he made his latest revelation to them. Then they rushed in to see how he had disposed of the animals and human images they had placed as sacrifices upon his altar, and hurried back to report in awe-stricken terms what the great god had shown them. That, says the world of today, is authority! Jesus' talk of security through truth and love, of winning the world by good will, is a sentimental dream. His contention that the world can run on the motive of service is the poetic fancy of a visionary. In this mood Nietzsche exclaims, "Jesus died too soon. He would have repudiated his doctrine if he had lived to my age."

To this charge of sentimentalism the gospel of Christ has one reply: Remember, you men who stand on the authority of the practical, that the world you now have on your hands is the world you have made by your methods. You were in control when two world wars swept the earth, each one promising to be the war that would end all war. You have had a free hand in the years since the Second World War, and the talk of the coming of a third has grown out of your policies. The bombs you made for purposes of security have brought only increasing panic, because you forgot that anything one nation can make other nations can match. It may be sentimental to suppose the world can be run for service, but the men who know no motive but maximum profits have been in control through the whole sickening series of panics, depressions, and inflationary crises. It is your way of running the world, not Jesus' way, that now brings us to our insecure hovering on the brink of destruction of civilization, if not the extinction of man.

If the way ahead is to have any hope, there is no longer room for the question: Which authority shall lead? Self-assertion has brought us to the edge of ruin. Only self-surrender can save us. "I say to you, Love your enemies" (Matt. 5:44) —this is not sentimental nonsense in an atomic age. "We . . . are . . . members one of another" (Rom. 12:5) —this is no poet's dream in an era of supersonic flight. "In honour preferring one another" (Rom. 12:10, K.J.V.) —this is no longer folly but may be the world's only salvation.

What do you make of the creed when it declares, "He ascended into heaven, and sitteth at the right hand of God the Father Almighty; from thence he shall come to judge the quick and the dead"? Is it not a vivid and utterly valid assertion of the authority of a living Christ? He is no longer a local teacher of a tiny nation. His truth is not subject to the changes of the times. He is universal. He speaks with finality. He is above the limitations of earth. In the picture language of the creed, "He ascended into heaven."

On our acceptance of the truth he uttered hang all our destinies. To defy or neglect him is to march toward destruction. In this the creed speaks with desperate literalness: Beyond resurrection stands judgment.

II

Not only the world's authority, but its complacency as well, is challenged by the resurrection fact. Provincialism had its heyday in Palestine. That tiny country, 150 miles from north to south and averaging only 50 miles in width, could not even achieve unity within itself but was divided three ways. Judea and Galilee looked askance at each other, and both shared a fierce hatred for Samaria. Rome knew the provincialism of power, and Jerusalem was cursed with the provincialism of self-righteous religion.

How much that world shared in common with modern isolationism! These people would have recognized kindred spirits in those who draw back from missionary effort or aid to undeveloped areas, saying, "We have to save America first."

In the name of such a world, "They went and made the sepulchre secure." But the last word belonged to one whom neither tomb nor boundaries could restrain, whose final commission to his disciples contained the marching order, "Go therefore and make disciples of all nations" (Matt. 28:19). It did not come as a new idea. He had always held the world in his heart. From the beginning his talk sprang from a world-wide out-look. Check a complete concordance of the Bible, and you will find that the references to the word "world" in the Old Testament fill less than half a column, while those in the New Testament—though it is only a third the size of the Old—require more than two columns. The older attitude was to think of Jerusalem or Judea or Israel or some nation or people; Christ's was to think of the world. He had the world in his heart. "The field is the world" (Matt. 13:38), he said. "God so loved the world." (John 3:16.) "Go into all the world." (Mark 16:15.)

What item on the agenda of our time can match the importance of learning how to live in one world? The title given to their book by a group of atomic scientists a few years ago is still true—*One World or None*. We cannot go on permanently dividing it into halves that live by menacing each other, without paying the price of final catastrophe. But long before we had the wit to dream of one world, Jesus had an-nounced it. "He [God] made from one every nation of men to live on all the face of the earth" (Acts 17:26) —Jesus inspired these words. "Members one of another"—Jesus planted that idea. "Go therefore and make disciples of all nations"—Jesus issued that com-mand.

Only in Christ can the differences among men be erased until a unified world becomes possible. On a bitter winter day an old man marched with a com-pany of miserable prisoners from one Japanese con-centration camp to another. Already he had known too many of these wretched marches. He thought back over his missionary career. He had so loved these gracious Japanese people! Must it all end now in death on the road? His strength was gone. He had not eaten since noon of the preceding day. The cold was sapping away his little remaining strength. It seemed he must collapse.

He begged the guard to let him fall out of the line and die in peace but only got the curt reply, "Walk on!" He walked, but it could not be for long. Again he begged, and again there were only those brutal words, "Walk on!" When he pressed the matter a third time, the guard replied again with a loud command, "Walk on!" Then, coming closer, he said under his breath, "For we are coming to my grandmother's house."

Whatever could that mean? the old man wondered. Presently the guard dropped out of line, hurried into a little house by the road, and came out quickly, holding something between his two hands. Approaching the old man, he ordered, "Hold your hands like mine," and then, slipping his hands inside the old man's, left there a hot potato. Bending close to the old man's ear, he said two familiar words, from the Communion liturgy—"Take, eat." Then, stepping back, he raised his voice in the old command, "Walk on!"

It was all plain to the old man. Gruff commands, because the youth feared his officers. But his heart was full of sympathy; and those familiar words, "Take, eat," could mean only one thing—the youth was a Christian. With a strength sustained not only by the warm food but also by the warmer courage the deed had awakened, the old man marched on. There was hope that the future held better things if the young men who would shape its destinies had caught that spirit from the Master.[2]

Only new men can make a new world. Jesus sent his disciples to save the world in the only way it can be saved: by "baptizing," which changes men's center of allegiance and transforms their nature; and by "teaching," which opens the mind to the reality of how deeply we do belong to one another.

"They went and made the sepulchre secure"—the world's provincialisms speak here. But, "Go therefore and make disciples of all nations"—this is history's answer; and the wise will accept the challenge.

III

The world's authority, its complacent provincialism —yes, and its sense of being left alone—must meet the challenge of the resurrection fact. There is wonder in the Gospel's closing line, "Lo, I am with you always" (Matt. 28:20). Two men walked wearily to Emmaus, but a third fell in step with them and restored their courage, quickened their hope, brought back the zest of life. "Lo, I am with you always." In Paul's last days he was so utterly alone that, writing to Timothy about his trial, he set down these desolate words: "No one took my part; all deserted me." "But," he added, "the Lord stood by me" (II Tim. 4:16-17). That changed everything! Not one

---

[2] This story is retold from one of the delightful sketches in Margaret T. Applegarth's *Men as Trees Walking* and is used by permission of Harper & Bros., publishers.

alone, but two together. "Lo, I am with you always."
David Livingstone, in the privations, loneliness, and
sometimes the panic of his hundreds of miles of lone
wrestling with the jungle track, came back to those
words for courage again and again—"Lo, I am with
you always." Not one, but two, and he could go on.
"I am with you always."

"Tell my brethren," said the living Christ, "to go
to Galilee, and there they will see me" (Matt. 28:10).
Galilee was the backland. It was far from the center of
political or cultural authority. It was the workaday
realm where these men plied their trade. It was home.
It was where common people worked at common
tasks with the common heartaches. Really, you and I
live in Galilee. Do you remember the lost word of
Jesus' they found on a fragment of papyrus dug up
from the sand of the Egyptian desert—"Lift the stone,
and you shall find me; cleave the wood, and there am
I"? Wherever faithful people go loyally about their
common tasks, no matter how burdened by the humdrum, that is where they meet their Lord. "Tell my
brethren to go to Galilee, and there they will see me."

"He is not here," the angel said. "He is not here;
for he has risen." (Matt. 28:6.) Beside every grave in
all the world you can hear this message. There is a
dear spot where you feel nearer than anywhere else
to one you have "loved long since and lost awhile";
for there you saw that dear form laid to rest. It is
precious to go there. But in the trees and the grass
the wind whispers, "Not here. Risen. Not here. Not
here!" And the whisper is a vindication of a universal
conviction. The half-savage primitives, burying their

loved dead with food for a journey and weapons of the hunt, have heard the whisper, "Not here. Risen." And the great scientist, laying his daughter to rest beneath a stone inscribed, "Nevertheless I live," has heard it. "Not here. Risen." The mind of the race believes that such a universal conviction has meaning. As the universal quests for food and light and fellowship and love and truth and meanings were not born to be mocked, but each has its satisfaction; so thoughtful men believe that the universal whisper, "Not here. Risen," is not an illusion but the pointer to reality. This glimpse of the living Lord is a vindication of what we cannot but believe.

Some of us know what it is to keep meeting the challenge of a Christ no grave can hold. We sink in our sins, and he challenges us with what we ought to be. We draw back from sin to remorse verging on despair, and he challenges us with the wonder of forgiveness and new life. Into our complacency with our little lives he comes with the disturbing vision of what he did with a brief thirty-three years and with the question of what we are doing with our years. We try to settle into a mere occupation, and he insists we have a calling. We come to the end of our resources, and he shows us how to live from great depths. We meet reverses, and he helps us to see that failure is but a stopping point on the way to victory if we let it drive us nearer to God. In the crucible of our intimate and intense experience we have tested the truth that Christ, crucified and resurrected, is the hope of the world.

5. Supposing We Cannot Experience God

I believe in the Holy Spirit . . .

Not long ago a student nearing graduation from one of our professional schools confessed his hopelessness of the possibility of having any direct experience of God. The only God he could believe in, he said, would be the force which brought into being the primordial electrons from which the world process evolved: after that initial act, the world went its independent way. Such a God might well exist, he said, but it was apparent that we could not know him.

A good many of us who might not put the case so extremely may well be equally hopeless concerning any real dealings with God. So widespread is this feeling that when a section of the Assembly of the World Council of Churches at Amsterdam attempted to set down the axioms from which the thinking of the modern man begins, one of them read, "There may be a God—but what does it matter?" By no means all those who share this sense of impotence to know God are irreligious people. The pastor of one distinguished American parish circulated a questionnaire on which 92 per cent of the answers indicated belief in God, although less than 50 per cent said they had ever felt his presence. Perhaps some of us are among that great number who, believing, feel themselves shut out from any firsthand experience.

To all such the Christian faith makes an amazing assertion. You can know God firsthand, it says, because it is the very nature of God to take the initiative in entering men's lives. This is the simple, direct meaning of what the Apostles' Creed—Christendom's ecumenical confession of faith—has to say about God. He is the creative, intelligent Purpose back of existence, the one abiding Reality, "God the Father Almighty, Maker of heaven and earth." But he is nearer to us than that; he comes into history in knowable form through Jesus Christ, in whom the eternal creative Mind "became flesh and dwelt among us," God's "only Son our Lord." Yes, adds the creed, but God comes even nearer than that. It is part of his eternal nature to be always going forth into the world, taking the initiative in intimate dealings with simple human beings; this is what Christendom means when in its devotions it confesses, "I believe in the Holy Spirit."

Not only so, but also our human nature is made for the experience of God. So far are we from being strangers to it that we require it if we are to live to the full. Our nature demands that we give allegiance to something, and our human problem is in part that we forever entangle ourselves in allegiance to something less than the highest. John Galsworthy portrayed all humanity through the moving drama he called *Loyalties,* in which a crime was committed and the characters then attempted to defend that to which each recognized allegiance—one, his family; another, his regiment; and others, a social set, a race, a business firm. With the best of intentions they were thus thrown into hopeless conflict. Finally one of them committed suicide, leaving a note which remarked, "A pistol keeps faith." Reading that sentence, one of the other characters paused to muse, "Keeps faith! We've all done that. It's not enough." Much of the pathos of our humanity is there. Made for a high allegiance, we give our loyalty away to something less than the highest; out of this springs our conflict.

Long ago Augustine went through all that in his own wayward experience, until at length he wrote a sentence so true that it has echoed through the thought and devotion of all the centuries since—"Thou hast made us for thyself, and our hearts are restless until they rest in thee." Do you suppose this is the story of some of us? Made in our very nature for a high allegiance, giving ourselves away to something less than the highest, left restless, uneasy, at odds with too much of the world, perhaps even at odds with ourselves—could that be our story: "Thou hast made us for thyself, and our hearts are restless until they rest in thee"?

Jesus, who read our human nature with an astuteness the ages cannot deny, and whose insight into the nature of God brings us to the pinnacle of all our religious knowledge, said all this unforgettably. "If a man loves me, he will keep my word, and my Father will love him, and we will come to him and make our home with him." (John 14:23.) As John remembered the conversation, Jesus identified this visitation with the Holy Spirit. Could it ever be said more plainly? God would come close enough to make his home with any who cared enough about him to keep his word!

64

If this really is literal truth for people like us, it is no small matter. Jesus predicted that such experience would bring counsel, clarity, understanding. Who of us does not need these? Isaiah declared the experience could bring a kind of stamina that lasts beyond the heat of a crisis, when what strength you have rises to the challenge and enables you to "mount up with wings like eagles" or to "run and not be weary," and sees you through drudging days of slogging along amid wearing difficulties with endurance to "walk and not faint" (Isa. 40:31). Who of us does not need this? And now a faith, tested by the tragedies and triumphs of too many people to be lightly dismissed, proclaims that God's nature and yours are so made for each other that you really can have this experience which counts more heavily than you can guess.

I

Some experiences which come to each of us bring us into contact with an order of reality that lies beyond the cold material world. There are moments of beauty when the landscape seems to be more than the sum of its clods and processes, as it reaches out mystic fingers to awaken in us a thrill of joy that we are convinced is more than a mere chemical response to a material environment. Or when we listen to a haunting phrase of music, the inner joy seems unmistakably more than an echo of vibrations on varying frequencies. Or in some high moment when a friend speaks so understandingly to our inner and unspoken need that we wonder how he knew, who does not feel that he is in touch with a world that transcends the material?

Niemöller, imprisoned to silence his gospel, writes to his wife about God's superb laughter when men think they can stop truth and faith so easily; they imprison a preacher, but the churches are then more crowded than ever, and the truth marches on! A friend commiserates Niemöller's father on the sorrow of having a son in prison, and he replies that it is indeed a sad experience but would be far more so if God needed a witness "and our Martin did not respond." Seeing men pay such a price for the freedom to say the truth, or seeing some lad fling himself into angry waters and lay down his own life to save another, who can doubt that he is standing close to an order of reality more than material?

Not all of us can say with Wordsworth, "I have felt a presence that disturbs me with the joy of elevated thoughts." It does not seem quite that personal. Yet there are spiritual experiences that come undeniably to each of us. The conscience that accuses us, not only of the wrong done but also of the duty neglected—who of us can escape that? The inner urgency that drives us to do, against our own protesting lethargy or fear, what finally we have to do or know no rest—who of us has not known that? And if we dismiss conscience as a mere result of long conditioning, there is still the fact that we are made with a *capacity* to respond so, and it seems to us beyond a doubt that in such moments we are dealing with something deeper than our glands and reflexes.

There is an experience that presents itself to us as more than material, in which out of anxiety and despair we come to some real peace. William James leaves traces of such an experience in his writings. There is an early letter in which as a young man he talks of his inner turmoil and even hints darkly at a struggle with thoughts of suicide. Then in one of the famous lectures delivered at Edinburgh he seems to recall such a moment as he says, "There is a state of mind known to religious men, but to no others, in which the will to assert ourselves and hold our own has been displaced by a willingness to close our mouths and be as nothing in the floods and waterspouts of God. . . . The time for tension in our soul is over, and that of happy relaxation, for calm deep breathing, or an eternal present with no discordant future to be anxious about, has arrived."

Beauty, friendship, a price paid for truth or freedom, the insistence of conscience, the emergence into peace—here are spiritual experiences known in some measure to all men, and none is so unmystical as to be denied a share in them. If, now, God were to come into your life, how else would you expect him to come than in such experiences as these? Creator and Sustainer of an orderly universe, would he come in spectacular interruptions of orderly life, or in that which brings it to its supreme climactic moments? Supreme Purposer, would he not come in the experiences that bring purpose to its decisive peaks? Everlasting Father, would he not meet us in the experiences that most mature and complete the development of his children?

Do you suppose it might be that some of us who think we cannot experience God have failed to recognize how near he has come to us, because we have been looking for him in some pattern too set and inflexible? If he is our Father, would he not approach his children, as a wise father would, in terms of their varying capacities and temperaments? Some of us have capacity and a bent for mystical experiences of what our Quaker friends call "the inner light"; but not all are so endowed. I once studied under a professor whose analytical mind was so keen that even his emotions seemed most aroused by a close-knit logical process well stated; and I have no doubt that his religious experiences, which came primarily through relentless reasoning, brought him into valid contact with God. Other friends I know meet him most recognizably through aesthetic experiences, in music or nature. Still others, without whom the world would be sadly impoverished, seldom have an emotional experience they can associate with God but are forever giving themselves in some form of practical service; and in these things they do, God comes close to them.

Perhaps you, too, in impressions that run far beyond the inert material surroundings from which they spring, have been having spiritual experiences of a depth and significance you have not recognized. You may even have been meeting God without knowing him.

II

For those who recognize such experiences and make a place for them, they can assume an importance utterly decisive. Anyone who has grappled seriously with real problems, and been attentive to his experience in the process, will have seen how the subconscious mind works. More than one noted mathematician has told the story of problems long faced in midnight wrestles, from which he turned at last in hopelessness and went to sleep leaving them unsolved, only to wake in the morning with the whole solution sharp and clear before him.

In a letter to Ralph W. Sockman, James Francis Cooke, former editor of *Etude,* described a somewhat related experience. In his sleep he dreamed of a musician who had been going about the musical circles of Florence boasting immoderately of his latest composition. Waking, he went directly to his desk and set down these lines as they came to him in the Italian language:

> The moment of triumph is always very dangerous,
> Because you believe that you have made
> Your book,
> Your picture,
> Your drama,
> Your symphony,
> Your victory,
> Poor fool! Poor fool!
> Do you not realize that you are merely
> The glove on the hand of God? [1]

What if our subconscious mind itself were merely "the glove on the hand of God"? Do you suppose we have ruled God out when we have given some psychological process a more complete description and a name?

Jesus led us to expect that in these quiet processes

[1] From: *How to Believe,* by Ralph W. Sockman. Copyright 1953 by Ralph W. Sockman, reprinted by permission of Doubleday & Company, Inc.

God would come to us with profound effects. "If you love me," he said, "you will keep my commandments. And I will pray the Father, and he will give you another Counselor, to be with you for ever, even the Spirit of truth." (John 14:15-17.) In the familiar words of the King James Version this visitation of God is spoken of as "another Comforter," but the Revised Standard Version translates it "Counselor" to help us remember that God's coming is not just to soothe. Phillips Brooks used to say that we ministers too often try to help people in their troubles by merely soothing them. And he went on, "The truest help which one can render to a man who has any of the inevitable burdens of life to carry is not to take his burden off but to call out his best strength that he may be able to bear it."

This kind of help is both counsel and comfort. A really good counselor helps us to see ourselves. The sight is not always pleasant, but it is often curative. There is no more decisive moment in Jesus' parable of the prodigal son than "when he came to himself." What he saw in himself was sickening, but it was the beginning of his healing. So a good counselor helps us to see ourselves. He also helps us to understand the real issues we are facing. He does not always tell us the answers, but he helps us to find them by helping us to see what are the real questions. There are many experiences that bring us to ourselves, sharpening the real issues; many moments of insight that bring us to deeper understanding and new beginnings. Do you suppose they may be "the glove on the hand of God"?

Recounting Paul's career, the book of Acts relates how he attempted to go to the promising cultural center, Bithynia, but was prevented. The door did not open. The record does not say exactly what happened, but the interpretation of the event is luminous. "They attempted to go into Bithynia," it reads, "but the Spirit of Jesus did not allow them; so, passing by Mysia, they went down to Troas." (Acts 16:7-8.) From the promising opportunities of Bithynia to the rough port city of Troas—what a disappointment that must have been! Would not most of us have centered our attention on the untoward circumstances that upset our plan? Not so Paul! It was no impersonal closed door. It was no mere hard luck. "The Spirit of Jesus did not allow them"! So, on to Troas with an open mind and an eager heart! No wonder Troas afforded a vision of one saying, "Come over to Macedonia and help us," and opened the door to previously undreamed opportunities. Do you suppose we miss the best things God has for us because we are blind to his coming in such unexpected circumstances? Could it be that even they are "the glove on the hand of God"?

To those who are ready God comes in ways utterly decisive. At a Communion service in the South Sea Islands a native Christian who had been a cannibal found himself kneeling at the altar next to a man who, years before, had killed his father, and against whom he had sworn vengeance. Overwhelmed with emotion, he returned to his seat without making his communion. But as he did so, the words of Jesus began to flash through his mind: "By this all men will know that you are my disciples, if you have love

71

for one another" (John 13:35). This was followed by a vision of the cross and an echo of the prayer, "Father, forgive them; for they know not what they do" (Luke 23:34). This settled the matter. With forgiveness in his own heart he went back to the altar.

What do you suppose made him remember exactly those things in a moment so tense? Could it have been as Jesus said, "The Counselor, the Holy Spirit, whom the Father will send in my name, he will teach you all things, and bring to your remembrance all that I have said to you" (John 14:26)? Are such moments "a glove on the hand of God"?

III

The Christian faith of the ages has held they are, and for some of us the advancing experience of the years only serves to confirm this reality. For some of us now, it all ought to come fresh and new. For, while the experience is available to us all, not all of us have entered in. As Aldous Huxley once remarked, "Experience is not what happens to a man; it is what a man does with what happens to him." So, to some of us here have happened events that provide materials for a profound experience of God; but we have something to do with them now that can make the mighty difference.

John Burroughs used to say that nature only unfolds her secrets to those who keep looking. "Not by a first casual glance, but by a steady deliberate aim of the eye, are the rarest things discovered. You must look intently and hold your eye firmly to the spot if you are to see more than do the rank and file of mankind." Those who have known God best have been sure it was equally true in experiencing his presence. You must pray without ceasing, Paul said—get the habit of prayer until it becomes the atmosphere of your life. There is a steady gaze at God that comes through yielded obedience. "If you love me, you will keep my commandments," said Jesus, adding that such obedience is the first step to the great experience of God's presence as the Counselor.

Supreme classic of men's experience of God is the New Testament story of Pentecost. Then the Holy Spirit came in a way that made weak men strong, uncertain men sure, hesitant men positive, timid men supremely courageous. But no reading of the story of Pentecost is adequate which misses the fact that these men had faced a demanding world task. The need of the world was on their heart. The demands of Christ tugged at their conscience. It has been well said that they received the pentecostal power when they faced a pentecostal task.

Professor William E. Hocking of Harvard once reported a luminous conversation with a psychiatrist friend. Said the psychiatrist,

Something has been occurring to me recently which seems important, and yet it is so simple that I can hardly believe it very significant. It is a way of taking the miscellany of events which make up the day's impressions of the world. One sees no trend in them. But suppose there were a trend which we cannot define but can nevertheless have an inkling of. There is certainly some direction in evolution, why not in history? If there were such a trend, then we men could be either with it or against it. To be with it would give a certain peace and settlement; to be against it would involve a subtle inner restlessness. To have confidence in it would be a sort of commitment, for better or for worse. I wonder if that is what you mean by religion.

When Professor Hocking answered in the affirmative, his friend asked, "Is that all there is to it?"

"I think that is the substance of it," Dr. Hocking replied. "The great religious ones seem to have had a certainty that they were going along with the trend of the world. They have had a passion for right living which they conceived of as a cosmic demand."

"There is nothing contrary to science in that," remarked the psychiatrist.

"No," said Professor Hocking, "but it makes a difference, doesn't it?" And his friend concluded the conversation, "Strange that such a simple thing should make so very much difference." [2]

It is for this simple, decisive thing that I plead now. It can come to all of us, and most of us have dealings with God more significant than we realize in our supposition that we cannot experience him. But we need not leave them to wayward chance. Through the cultivation of the habit of prayer, through the disciplines of obedience to the highest we know, through the acceptance of some real part of the world's load, confronting vital issues and others' needs, we can rediscover what countless others have found true: the God who deals with us even when we do not recognize him will bring new floods of peace and power into the lives that consciously open the door to his entrance. Strange, indeed, that such a simple thing should make so very much difference!

[2] *What Man Can Make of Man,* by William E. Hocking. Used by permission of Harper & Bros., publishers.

6. Wanting Christ Without Christianity

... the holy catholic Church, the communion of saints ...

It is not uncommon to meet men and women of good will who, honoring Christ, wanting more of his quality of life to spread through society, nevertheless hold aloof from any real part in the Christian fellowship which enlists men in loyalty to him. George Bernard Shaw made himself their spokesman when he wrote, "I am no more of a Christian than Pilate was ...; and yet ... I am ready to admit that I see no way out of the world's misery but the way which would have been found by his will." Shaw, with his penetration of the mind of his time, even dared to identify his reader with this point of view.

One meets those for whom Shaw spoke—holding Christ in high regard even while they remain aloof from any personal commitment—frequently enough to suppose there may be some of them among us now. To these unquestionably high-minded friends I wish I might have the privilege of saying a simple, sincere word.

I

You are right in reverencing Christ, my friend. He has won the allegiance of towering personalities of amazingly different turns of mind in widely scattered lands—Tolstoy the Russian, Schweitzer the Alsatian,

Livingstone the Briton, Pascal the Frenchman, Kierke-gaard the Dane, and Kagawa the Japanese, coming over their diverse roads of humane letters, artistic intuition, daring exploration, scientific research, critical philosophy, and utterly selfless human service to meet around his throne.

Not only do his disciples supplement one another. His critics cancel each other out, as one brands him a "fanatic" while another scorns him as "too indul-gently mild"; one calls him "lacking in artistic genius" while another dismisses him because of the supposed unreality of his "impossibly beautiful dreams"; or one brands him "too feminine" even while another com-plains that he is "too rigorously demanding." [1]

Not by virtue of his advantages but in defiance of all obstacles, his influence reaches us. Misunderstood by his family, who thought him demented and sought to restrain him; excommunicated by his own house-hold of faith, which branded him a heretic; betrayed by his intimate friends, who failed him in his greatest need; crucified by his nation, which placed upon him the brand of treason; bitterly opposed by the Roman Empire, which used its fiercest persecutions in the at-tempt to blot out his memory, he still towers over twenty centuries with an influence so pervasive that Emerson declared his name was not so much written as plowed into history. You are right in revering him; for there is no other remotely like him.

Have you considered, however, how empty a rever-ence for Christ that remains uncommitted to any personal allegiance to him can be? It will not do to

[1] Cf. George Buttrick, in *The Interpreter's Bible*, VII, 449, 451.

hold this position in the name of keeping an open mind. It is not always a mark of maturity to maintain an open mind. When your country struggles for its life, it will not satisfy honor to say that as between this country and its enemies you will not commit yourself to a decision, but prefer rather the impartiality of an open mind. As democracy and human rights grapple with totalitarian communism, it is not enough to say that as an open-minded intellectual you prefer to remain uncommitted to either. There are unexplored or partially known areas in the sciences in which the noncommittal position of open-minded waiting is a mark of maturity; but about the embattled issues men must live with, Gilbert K. Chesterton spoke the deeper truth when he declared, "I am incurably convinced that the object of opening the mind, as of opening the mouth, is to shut it again on something solid."

Do you suppose it is enough to admire a Christ whose way of life is under fierce attack, yet remain uncommitted to him? For the overwhelming majority of the world's 700,000,000 Christians, of all sorts and communions, there is a commitment which they express through the words of the creed the greatest number of them hold in common: "I believe in . . . the holy catholic Church, the communion of saints." In this expression of allegiance they give themselves to a Christ who is more than a historical memory, an abstract idea, or a mystical experience; they give themselves to a Christ who becomes concretely tangible in a living fellowship of faith and loyalty. Paul was speaking of such commitment to a Christianity of real and immediate loyalties when, writing of Christ to the Ephesians, he said, "He [God] has put all things under his feet and has made him the head over all things for the church, which is his body" (Eph. 1:22-23). Coming to this theme again in his letter to the Colossians, he put it tersely: "He is the head of the body, the church" (1:18).

This is no petty church to which Paul and the creed have reference. It is more than a local parish or a denomination; more than some great branch, as Protestantism, Roman Catholicism, Eastern Orthodoxy. It is universal—which is what the word "catholic," in its original sense, means. It sweeps beyond the confines of this world and this time and includes all committed followers of Christ—both those on earth and those in heaven—in "the communion of saints." Yet, all-embracing as it is, it is vividly real, so that those who live within this fellowship are possessed by an abiding loyalty and have become a part of that company who not only seek their own salvation, but also have put themselves at the disposal of Christ's spirit for the carrying out of his will and the doing of his work in this world of urgently immediate realities.

To some friend who, despite his unquestioned respect for the personality of Christ, has been standing outside the organized Christian fellowship, tolerantly acknowledging that the Church probably does no harm, I wish I might bring home the realization that it is through the Church that the spirit, influence, and work of Christ come to the world; so that for those who honor him and who believe there is need for more of his quality of life, there is no room for benevolent neutrality, but rather an urgent call to committed allegiance.

II

To think of the Church as the body of Christ is to use a figure of speech which passes beyond metaphor to the literal reality that it is through this body of loyal devotion that Christ's spirit and influence find their continuing expression in the world. Ask yourself this question: How did I come to know this Christ whose name I hold worthy of admiration? Was it not, first of all, through the Bible—either your own reading of it or secondhand reports from others who had read it? While there are some primary sources of historical knowledge of him outside the Bible, by all odds the fullest accounts are found in the New Testament documents. But whence came the Bible, save from the Church, in the midst of whose fellowship and as a part of whose life and witness these records were set down, preserved, translated, circulated, and given currency in the world?

For those who pass beyond hearsay to the knowledge of Christ that comes as friend lives with Friend in faith's consecration, it is the Church which leads the way to such commitment. And for those who come to that fullest knowledge which accrues only through venturing with him in loyal service, it is the Church which affords the channels for the most fruitful ventures and issues the call to enlistment.

As in personal experience, so is it in history. Listen, for instance, to the two ringing sentences with which Will Durant concludes the discussion of "The War of

Church and State" in his massive study *Caesar and Christ:*

> There is no greater drama in human record than the sight of a few Christians, scorned and oppressed by a succession of emperors, bearing all trials with a fierce tenacity, multiplying quietly, building order while their enemies created chaos, fighting the sword with the word, brutality with hope, and at last defeating the strongest state that history had known. Caesar and Christ had met in the arena, and Christ had won.

His victory had been, to be sure, the triumph of his spirit, the march of irresistible truth in his ideas, the vindication of his name by the irrefutable validity of all he stood for; but it was no disembodied victory. Gibbon might dismiss his followers with the scornful judgment that "Christians were almost entirely composed of the dregs of the populace, of peasants and mechanics, of boys and women, of beggars and slaves"; but it was through these obscure people, banded together in the committed fellowship which, as another historian said, "out-lived, out-thought, and out-died the pagan world," that Christ's spirit carried on and won its way.

As in personal experience and in history, so is it in the geographic extension of Christ's influence among earth's teeming populations. Those who admire Christ and believe his influence a good thing must never forget that this influence, far from a simple accident one can casually take for granted, proceeds under the challenge of many powerful rivals. On a planet where there are a round 350,000,000 Confucianists and Taoists, 315,000,000 Mohammedans, 256,-

000,000 Hindus, 150,000,000 Buddhists, 11,000,000
Jews, and nearly 500,000,000 who espouse other faiths
or remain outside any, how do you suppose Christ—
whose influence spread from the smallest and least
populous nations—has won 742,000,000 followers?
There can be but one answer: through the gallant missionary enterprise of the Christian Church.

It was the Church which saw that his teachings were
translated and circulated in more than a thousand
languages and dialects. It was the missionaries of the
Church who for the purpose of spreading his word
first gave written form to hundreds of languages never
before reduced to writing. It was the Church which
translated his teachings not only into words but also
into the selfless deeds of a great army of teachers, agri-
culturalists, medical missionaries, and other techni-
cians who at gallant personal risk carried on vital
technical-assistance programs long before govern-
mental agencies entered the field or today's vital
official programs of aid to underdeveloped areas were
dreamed of.

A careful historian like Kenneth Scott Latourette
puts compactly the story of how Christ's influence
has won its wide geographical permeation when he
observes that through the world mission of the Church
it has been carried onto more frontiers, by more
agents, supported by more funds, given by more small
donors, than ever represented any other idea.

Christ's reach into personal lives, the march of his
spirit and influence through the embattled centuries,
and his progress across the world have come through
one single agency—his Church. These are the things

we mean when we call the Church his "body"; and these vital tasks comprise the urgency underlying the claim that for those who honor him and think his influence worth while, there can be no neutrality, but only a place within the committed fellowship.

III

To think of the Church as Christ's body is to recognize a second truth: Through this body one comes into the most helpful contact with his living spirit. No sane person would suppose that when Jesus taught in Galilee, his body was unimportant. It was through his body that he found a voice and that his thoughts shaped themselves into words whose truth changed lives, and echoes through the centuries. It was his helpful hand that was placed under more than one heavy load of loneliness or sickness, his weary feet that carried him from one place of need to another. When at last he came to teach his ultimate lesson of sacrificial love, he passed beyond words altogether, and "threw his body in," to die on a cross.

As his physical body served to bring his spirit into most helpful contact with persons he would reach, so he looked forward to the fellowship of those committed to his service to bring him into contact with need in days to come. Despite all the disagreements of historical research concerning the authenticity of the details of the passage, Matthew seems undoubtedly to have been remembering some actual saying of Jesus' when he wrote, "On this rock I will build my church, and the powers of death shall not prevail against it. I will give you the keys of the kingdom of heaven, and whatever you bind on earth shall be bound in heaven, and whatever you loose on earth shall be loosed in heaven" (Matt. 16:18-19). Underlying all varying interpretations, one bedrock truth is here: Christ foresaw in his church a vital agency for bringing his spirit into most helpful touch with those who need him.

That he was not thinking of the Church as founded on any such crumbling rock as Peter proved to be seems plain enough. Before the incident was finished, Jesus had turned on Peter as "Satan"; had said, "You are a hindrance to me"; had called him, "not on the side of God, but of men." (Matt. 16:23.) The rock on which Jesus could build was rather the *faith* Peter had confessed, that Jesus is "the Christ, the Son of the living God" (Matt. 16:16). Wherever this faith binds men together, there the Church exists; and where this faith is lacking, whatever else men have, they lack the essential element on which to build the Church. Even with men as weak and failing as Peter proved to be on more than one occasion, a fellowship bound together by this faith is irresistible.

It is this faith which binds the allegiance of the Church. Great numbers of men outside the Church to-day will tell you, "Jesus was a good man. What we need are a lot more people like him." Yet it is not these casual admirers, who eulogize his human goodness, who most spread his influence in the world. When, early in American history, the Congregational Church divided into two branches, one of which held that Jesus is "the Christ, the Son of the living God," and the other, that he is a good man and what we need are a lot more like him; it might have been

83

reasonable to suppose that Christ's influence would spread farthest through those who took the humanly reasonable approach to the molding of human character in his image; but such has not been the case. Whatever else may be said for the latter branch—the Unitarian Societies—no claim can be made that it has become a numerous group. The influence of Christ has not spread principally through those who thought it a simple matter of wishing for a lot more people like him, but through those who in committed allegiance allowed him to touch their lives with a transforming influence. Where men stand thus committed, they are generally found within the body of the Church.

In a day when people live in silent dread of the anonymous authority of public opinion; when men and women are shaped in spite of themselves in the image of a nameless average, feeling compelled to be just like everybody else in their style of clothing, their automobile, and their political opinions; when this gravitation to the dead average menaces freedom and limits the prospect of creative living, it is more than ever vital that we build a strong fellowship of those so committed to another and higher Authority that through their fellowship his saving touch may be laid on individuals and society. Won't you come and help us to that high end?

IV

To think of the Church as Christ's body, finally, is to see it as an organic whole, within whose unity the many different parts fall into place as important, not in themselves, but in what they mean within the living wholeness of the body. Paul kept coming back to this truth. Eyes, ears, hands, feet, cannot go it alone! They must contribute to the welfare of the body, and in turn depend on its total health. So, he said, with Christians in the Church—it depends upon them, yet it is only through its life and health that they live to the full.

I wish we might face the implications of this now. Within this fellowship we bear each other's burdens; yet though the Church calls us to be burden bearers, our own load of sorrow or loneliness or failure is best borne within this devoted company. The Church proclaims the world's highest standard of morality and expects its members to help uphold this standard; yet its doors are open wide to men and women who know themselves to be sinners, and, indeed, it is the one fellowship in the world which admits men and women to membership for the one reason that they are needy sinners. No one should be kept out of the Church by a modesty that supposes oneself unworthy or by a sincerity that scorns the hypocrisy of espousing a standard too high, for the Church is comprised not of those who claim perfection, but of those who know their need of help to a higher level of life.

Within the unity of this body our differences find their best chance of healing. For differences of opinion, really devoted life within this fellowship is the best solvent. No real church grows by settling differences as they are settled within a club, by cliques and factions. No real church life emerges from the pressure methods of a political organization. Wherever a church seeks to settle its differences in these ways, it ceases by so much to be the Church, and defeats its own ends. Within the one body of the Church even difference of race and nationality becomes insignificant, for we are all one in Christ Jesus.

If you tell me you must hold aloof because the church does not live up to these standards, I would reply that I too know its failures—its bigotries, its lethargy about important matters and its petty devotion to trivial concerns, its party strifes, its racial discriminations. Yet despite them all, I believe it is the one hope of bringing Christ's saving touch to the world; and I appeal to you to come and help us make it what it ought to be.

7. Can Yesterday
Be Changed?

. . . the forgiveness of sins . .

Who has not asked himself, concerning some choice he has made or deed he has done, "Why, oh, why, did I do that?" Or who has not said, in tones of wistfulness, "If I could only have that moment to live over again, how different everything would be!" If only wishing made it so! But there is no setting back the clock. What has passed into history is irretrievable.

> The Moving Finger writes; and, having writ,
> Moves on: nor all your Piety nor Wit
>   Shall lure it back to cancel half a Line,
> Nor all your Tears wash out a Word of it.

Yet living at peace with our yesterdays remains a problem which we try to solve by a variety of devices. "Let bygones be bygones," we say, hoping to close the door on unpleasant yesterdays and seal them off. Some things there are, however, which we cannot forget, try as we will. "There's no use crying over spilled milk," we tell ourselves; yet some regrets do linger, and our brave maxims cannot drive them off. Borrowing a term from the psychologists, we say, "I'll simply have to accept myself; this is how I am, and how I must be." But there are some aspects of ourselves, and especially of what we know is unworthy in our yesterdays, which by slow stages we learn we cannot live with or accept until we have dealt with them in some other way.

For dealing with these troublesome yesterdays, Christianity has a cardinal principle, so central to the Christian faith and life that it is among the slender handful of basic realities gathered up into the creed used by the great majority of the world's Christians of all communions, and stated in a few swift words: "I believe in . . . the forgiveness of sins."

We live in a period which does not talk as much about this doctrine as Christians once did; so that a volume published as the "best sermons" of a recent year, selected by a distinguished interfaith committee, does not even list the word "forgive" in its index. "Faith" is there; and "Freedom," with a long list of references; and a host of other words beginning with "F"—but not "Forgive."

Whether we keep the word in our working vocabulary or not, we have no way of dismissing it from our needs; and what to do with yesterdays that cannot be silenced remains among our problems. The great spiritual tradition we have inherited is full of awareness of this need, so that the religious experiences reflected in the Bible persistently deal with it. "Though your sins are like scarlet, they shall be as white as snow," Isaiah assures us. (Isa. 1:18.) Jesus teaches us to pray,

> Forgive us our debts,
> As we also have forgiven our debtors (Matt. 6:12);

and as if to prove that none are beyond the reach of this plea, he prays from the cross, "Father, forgive

them; for they know not what they do" (Luke 23:34).
John, completing the cycle, writes in his First Epistle,
"If we confess our sins, he is faithful and just, and
will forgive our sins and cleanse us from all unrighteousness" (1:9).

The mind of our time, unable to accept ideas on
the basis of tradition, cannot but ask, "Is all this real?
What is forgiveness? Can it change yesterday in any
way that matters?" I wish we might examine these
questions quite simply together, for they are important. If nothing about yesterday can be changed, a
great deal of the Christian faith is nonsense. If it can,
the fact is so important for our personal welfare and
mental health and the peace of the world that no one
of us can afford to neglect it.

I

See, then, what a range of familiar experiences con-
spires to underline the truth that yesterday not only
can be changed, but is changed, again and again. For
one thing, it changes in its meaning for us. A yesterday that has been a nightmare in our memories can
be flooded with what Paul called "the peace . . . which
passes all understanding" (Phil. 4:7). One practicing
psychologist tells the story of a tiny lad who had been
the victim of dreams in which a fierce tiger appeared,
night after night, until the little fellow feared to go
to sleep. The psychologist sat at the lad's bedside as
he was going to sleep, and told him about the tiger
he would be seeing—a friendly tiger he need not
fear. "Just put out your hand and pet him, and say,
'Hello, old chap,'" the counselor told him. As his
parents later watched beside him, the boy presently

began to toss in his sleep, with the familiar signs of the approaching dream. But then he relaxed, and as one little hand moved as if to stroke a pet, he half muttered, "Hello, old chap," and with a smile slept on in peace.

So yesterday can change its meaning for us. Yet we cannot make peace with what has been by make-be-lieve, but only by an honesty which faces our past selves and finds the relaxation that forgiveness brings. This reality is a simple matter of record in the experience of countless men and women.

No honest soul could long live at peace with an unworthy yesterday, however, if it were not true that yesterday can be changed in other ways as well. Consider how completely it can be changed in its effect on others. Not long ago I met a successful young physician who, after years of drinking, had come to the conclusion that alcohol is a costly evil, and that the social drinking which had not greatly hurt him had deeply damaged others in his circle, so that his influence had contributed to their undoing. Carrying the conviction into action, he made a clean break with the drink habit. Now he continues in the old circles, even stopping in at the bars he formerly frequented, proudly ordering soft drinks and using the record of the yesterdays as a background for his present witness against the drinks he once shared with the group. Much there is about those yesterdays that cannot be called back, yet much of their present effect on the lives of his friends has been totally transformed.

When this happens—as happen it does, again and again, in the struggles of men against all sorts of evils that have tarnished their records—it is forgiveness that opens the way to the changing of yesterday's effects.

Not only in its meaning to us and its effect on others, but also in the nature of the personal relations that characterized it, yesterday can be changed. A news story during the Second World War reported a dinner at an officers' mess in the R.A.F., at which the British fliers entertained as their guest a German pilot one of them had forced down. As a brave man, enemy that he was, he had won their respect. As they dined together, he broke into tears, and then after an embarrassing moment, is reported to have said: "Please forgive me. Your kindness has overwhelmed me. For most of my life I have been taught to dislike the English. For these last five years I have been made to hate them. I was told that if the English captured me, they would starve and torture me. Instead you have broken me with your kindness. Gentlemen, I salute you."

There have been abundant instances in which the relationships of strong men, once enemies, have been completely transformed. Not least of such is the American flier under Doolittle who, after release from a Japanese prison, returned to Tokyo to give his life in missionary service among his former enemies. When yesterday's relationships undergo such change, it is forgiveness which stands at the turning point.

In its outcomes yesterday can be changed, so that not infrequently one sees good emerging from what in the beginning was only evil. When the International Tribunal at The Hague declared in favor of the United States, exacting a large indemnity from the government of China for the American lives and

91

property lost in the Boxer uprising, our government did a surprising thing. Wise statesmen led us to hold these funds in trust for the education in American universities of promising young Chinese leaders, and all through the years that investment served to cement the relations of the United States and China. For many years the whole Orient was turned in friendship toward our country, as a good result of what was in the beginning only evil.

As our relations with Asia move in a sadly different atmosphere, the moral insights of that earlier period are still our most dependable guide. If we do not allow the fears and resentments of this desperate period to turn us from the policies that through the years have represented the heart of America at its best, we can still emerge with friends and an assured place in the world. Of one thing we may be sure: When an evil yesterday opens the way to surprisingly good outcomes, you will find that at the turning point there has always been some creative act of forgiveness.

Even what yesterday has made of us personally can be changed, as Professor Hocking of Harvard pointed out when, in his great study of *Human Nature and Its Remaking,* he declared:

Of all animals, it is man in whom heredity counts for least, and conscious building forces for most. Consider that his infancy is longest, his instincts least fixed, his brain most unfinished at birth, his powers of habit-making and habit-changing most marked, his susceptibility to social impressions keenest. . . . To anyone who asserts as dogma that "Human nature never changes," it is fair to reply, "It is human nature to change itself."

What the distinguished scholar thus asserts, Christianity has demonstrated again and again, as when in a single generation men move from illiterate headhunters to characters of such nobility and kindness that more than one GI has come home from some Pacific island to tell how the natives he met there taught him what it is to be a real Christian.

In its meaning within our own minds, its effect on others, its transformed human relations, its outcome of good from what started as only evil, even in what it makes of us, yesterday not only *can* be changed, but *is* changed in ways so vital as to give undeniable content to John's assertion, "If we confess our sins, he [God] is faithful and just, and will forgive our sins and cleanse us from all unrighteousness" (I John 1:9).

II

This truth, with which we have been dealing as if it were a proposition of only general interest, far from that, is of the most personal urgency to each of us. For who among us does not know in his heart some yesterdays that stand in need of change? As Harry Emerson Fosdick once put it, there is the disturbing fact that you are getting to be you! Some traits of character, some habits, some outlooks which characteristically color all you think and do, are so fastening themselves upon you that, whether you see it or not, your friends see you developing at some points in ways they can only regret.

We can scarcely dismiss this deepening set of our lives by saying that these, after all, are little things that do not matter. Rip Van Winkle, as Joseph

Jefferson dramatically portrayed him, excused each alcoholic dereliction by saying, "I won't count this time"; but, as William James wrote of him, "Down among his nerve-cells and fibers, the molecules are counting." For some of us this fact that what we are getting to be is tightening its grip upon us is now becoming crucial.

With some aspects of yesterday we can deal directly by our own decisive act. The king in Shakespeare's *Hamlet* is facing such realities when he soliloquizes:

> My fault is past. But, O! what form of prayer
> Can serve my turn? 'Forgive me my foul murder'?
> That cannot be; since I am still possess'd
> Of those effects for which I did the murder,
> My crown, mine own ambition, and my queen.
> May one be pardon'd, and retain the offence?

Clearly, the answer to this question must be, No! There are parts of yesterday we can and must deal with by our own act—a decisive break, in which we do all that lies within our power to correct the wrong we have done.

Yet there are deeds we can never overtake. Men in the Congress of the United States who have used their conspicuous place and congressional immunity to damage the reputations of others could not, even if they repented of their great evil, undo the damage they have done. Their lies have traveled into corners where no correction will ever reach. They have created suspicion and division among their countrymen at a time when unity is most needed, and suspicion once planted does not quickly die. They have so depressed the standard of truth in our public life that their lifetime will not see it lifted to the level from which they dragged it. They have taken the hard-won principle of justice, that a man is innocent until proved guilty, and perverted it into its ugly opposite, that a man is guilty until proved innocent.

What has been done conspicuously by evil men, perverting their power, happens again and again in our personal lives. The evil has run so far beyond our reach that our attempts to correct it can never overtake it. Our word has lodged in places we shall never guess. People we have injured have passed beyond the gates of death. Yesterday can no longer be changed by any act of ours.

How, then, shall we deal with it? No counsel to "forget it" reaches the depths of our need. When a man is suffering with some mental turmoil, the psychiatrist does not tell him to forget it! He probes deeper and helps the man remember more and more. Yesterday cannot be shrugged off; it must be faced. Only as we recall it and make peace with it, can we live in health. As in the troubles of the mind, so also in those of the spirit, yesterday must be faced; and for the yesterday that has passed beyond the reach of any deed of ours, forgiveness at the hands of God is the only way that holds hope. We have injured something more than an individual. We have done that which damaged the moral standard of the whole community. Only One who represents that widest moral standard can forgive us.

How happily for us, he is a forgiving God! Jesus pictured him in the story of a prodigal son and a loving father. The boy did not find his way out of his plight when he simply pitied himself for the consequences he had brought upon himself. But when he came to himself and saw that he had sinned against his father as well, the solution began to emerge. When he went home with his humble apology, he found his father waiting, watching, running down the road to meet him. Before he had even finished the prepared apology, the forgiveness was given. And that, Jesus said, is the everlasting truth about God. Some of us could enter into a new epoch in our lives if we would act now on an old assurance, so often tried and verified that it has become a universal law: "If we confess our sins, he is faithful and just, and will forgive our sins and cleanse us from all unrighteousness."

III

One word of warning should be said before we leave this truth that yesterday can be changed. There is no hope of changing it for those who are not themselves willing to forgive. Once and again one sees a man, with a lawsuit or some other form of vengeance, destroy the very thing he set out to protect. As the Second World War drew to a close, two eminent American statesmen, Herbert Hoover and Hugh Gibson, jointly published a penetrating study of *The Problems of Lasting Peace,* in which they concluded a chapter of vital inferences from diplomatic history by saying, "This endless treadmill of punishment must be stopped in the world if there is to be real peace. Victory with vengeance is ultimate defeat in the modern world. We can have peace or we can have revenge, but we cannot have both." Only the forgiving can be forgiven, for only they really believe in forgiveness.

Within the Christian church the unforgiving spirit is disastrously damaging. Do you remember that distinguished Norwegian novel *The Great Hunger,* in which a man whose child had been killed by a neighbor's dog lived only for revenge, until at last he learned there was no comfort in it? Then, in the midst of a famine that left the neighbor with no seed for his field, he went out in the dead of night and planted it with corn, explaining, "I sowed seed in my enemy's field that God might exist." His act did not create God. The Eternal was not dependent upon a man. But his deed opened the way to God's existence *for him.* Until he did it, he had barred the door to God and to any peace in his own soul.

For those of us who care about God, this is the awful truth. Within a Christian circle it sometimes happens that the unforgiving heart blocks the way for God's entrance, and only forgiveness can let him in. When, during World War II, the ministers in Shanghai's Japanese mission asked for the use of the Allen Memorial Church, oldest Methodist church in China, for worship by Japanese soldiers stationed in the city, the Chinese Christians hesitated, and then, after praying about the matter, granted the permission, because, they said, "We would not want the world to hear that the doors of our church had been closed to any group that wanted to worship God." Ah, but how often even the church is injured by the unforgiving spirit of those within it! The tragedy is not only that they shut out one another but also that they shut out God. For some of us, forgiveness of our brother, alone, will let God in; and this is the indispensable key to the saving of yesterday.

97

8. To Believe That Spirit Triumphs

. . . the resurrection of the body, and the life everlasting.

The minister sat at the bedside of a friend for whom death was not far away. "Tell me," said the man, "if you were in my place, knowing that presently you were to pass through those gates, what would you expect to find?" Quietly, then they thought together of their expectations concerning what, admittedly, "Eye hath not seen, nor ear heard, neither have entered into the heart of man" (I Cor. 2:9, K.J.V.).

What was necessary to that man, preparing for a great change, is important to us all. Young men in military service must make some terms with death, and the youth is fortunate who has arrived at a clear conception of its meaning, a faith in what lies beyond its opening door. Little by little a pastor learns that it is not the morbid alone who ask these questions, but that vigorous, healthy-minded youth share an eager quest for the answers. Who can live competently without some adequate grasp of where life leads in the end?

Since bereavement comes to each of us, the question of what lies beyond for those we love is vital even to those who profess no curious concern for themselves. Wordsworth expressed one possibility for those we have laid to rest:

> No motion has she now, no force;
>   She neither hears nor sees;
> Roll'd round in earth's diurnal course,
>   With rocks, and stones, and trees.

Is this inertness, made a part of the unthinking, unfeeling earth, all that is in store for the fair spirits who have slipped from us? At best, bereavement is an aching emptiness for the lonely hearts left behind, which Sir Walter Scott put eloquently after his wife's death, as he wrote, "A kind of cloud of stupidity hangs about me, as if all were unreal that men seem to be doing and talking." How doubly agonizing is this experience for those to whom death's door opens on nothing beyond!

Those who live by the Christian faith are not left in that plight. Nothing about Christianity more startled the pagan world than the quiet peace with which Christians faced death, for themselves and those they loved. Their startled surprise still lingers in the second century, as Aristides writes: "And if any righteous man among them passes from the world, they rejoice and offer thanks to God; and they escort his body as if he were setting out from one place to another near." Something of that amazement lingers even into our time, as once and again we see noble parents mark the passing of a loved child as if it were a commencement or an Easter celebration.

In this Christians follow a Master who lifted faith in eternal life out of the realm of remote generalities. To him it was no far-off matter of "the sweet bye and bye," no "beautiful Isle of Somewhere." To Martha, whose brother Lazarus had died, Jesus said, "Your

brother will rise again" (John 11:23). Martha, confident of some far-off rising, replied, "I know that he
will rise again in the resurrection at the last day"
(11:24). This, however, was not enough for Jesus.
"I am the resurrection and the life," he assured her.
"He who believes in me, though he die, yet shall he
live, and whoever lives and believes in me shall never
die" (11:25-26). So, he seemed to be saying, life is
not interrupted. Our loved ones do not die, to remain
long in a suspended, inanimate state from which they
may rise at some distant day. "Whoever lives and believes in me," said Jesus, "shall never die."

So central has this been to Christian faith that the
closely packed creed, of only a trifle more than one
hundred words, in which Christendom reviews its
basic principles, culminates in the affirmation, "I believe in . . . the resurrection of the body, and the life
everlasting." Now and again one meets men of good
will and true spirit who share the Christian outlook
in most regards but have difficulty with this article
of faith. I wonder how it is with you?

> "Are ye able" when the shadows
>   Close around you with the sod,
> To believe that spirit triumphs,
>   To commend your soul to God? [1]

If you were to pass soon through the gates of death,
have you any clearly thought conception of what you
might reasonably expect to find? Because this question is important to us all, will you examine it with
me?

[1] "Are Ye Able." Used by permission of Earl Marlatt.

100

I

Beyond death's door shall we not expect, first of all, that life continues? Our attempts to describe what it is like in its surroundings are admittedly inadequate. We cannot speak of such things without using some of the language of imagery. Yet necessarily all our images are drawn from earthly life. Can they in any sense correspond to life on another level of existence?

When the book of Revelation pictures streets of gold, gates consisting of one huge pearl, city walls studded with jewels, no thoughtful reader supposes this was meant as a literal picture of heaven. What it does present is an imaginatively appealing picture of a life full of completeness, security, victory. Presented as abstractions, these make little appeal to the heart; so that here in a book which has so appealed that it has outlived the centuries, we find them in the imagery of the poet, which is always concrete and always symbolic. We make our poetic pictures as best we can, but we do believe in the reality of life that knows no end.

We believe it because a universal human experience seems to argue for its truth. Wherever nature presents a universal yearning, it supplies the means of its fulfillment; so that we learn to reason that the yearning is itself an echo of the reality to which it corresponds. The eye develops in response to light; the ear, in adaptation to sound. For the universality of hunger there is food; for the desire for companionship there is a corresponding need in other people. What nature plants in all men as a yearning invariably reflects a corresponding reality in our environment.

When we discover in all races and tribes a universal

hunger for a life beyond—no tribe so primitive that its customs do not reflect this craving—we cannot but believe that nature, here as elsewhere, plants the longing in the heart as an echo of the reality to which it answers.

We believe in life's continuance because we believe in the conservation of energy. In the world around us we see energy constantly changing, but not lost. We see motion change into heat or heat into motion. We see mechanical energy expended as electrical energy is generated. We see electricity give rise to power or light or sound. Change is all about us, so that our world is made of the ceaseless interplay of changing forces. But physicists tell us that with all the change, no energy is ever lost. We cannot believe that a universe as reasonable as this one seems to be, can so carefully conserve physical energies and at the same time prodigally waste spiritual energies. Believing that personality is the highest fruitage of the universe, we find it incredible that a universe characterized by conservation on lower levels would squander its final product.

We believe that life goes on victoriously because this faith best harmonizes with the total pattern of the things we hold most certain. For we believe that God is love, and we cannot believe that a loving God would plant the yearning for immortality in the hearts of his children only to frustrate it. We believe that God's kingship of the world is a reality, and we cannot believe that his rule stops at any finite boundary as arbitrary as death. We believe that spirit is a reality deeper than matter, and we cannot believe that a little rebellious matter—a stray bullet, a particle in the throat causing strangulation, the growth of some minute germ—can cause the final defeat of spirit. We believe the spiritual values—truth, beauty, goodness—are of ultimate importance: and we cannot believe that when the last mortal eyes look upon this world, these values will cease to exist—which would be the case if there were no minds to know and no personality to cherish them.

We believe in the continuity of life because Jesus believed it. In all matters of the spirit his perceptions are keener, his mind wiser, his spirit ventures farther than any other. He has paid the greatest price to know. He speaks with the most dependable authority. And for him eternal life is as real and unarguable as the life we now have. "In my Father's house are many rooms," he says; "if it were not so, would I have told you that I go to prepare a place for you? And when I go and prepare a place for you, I will come again and will take you to myself, that where I am you may be also." (John 14:2-3.) To grieving friends he speaks with assurance, "I am the resurrection and the life; he who believes in me, though he die, yet shall he live, and whoever lives and believes in me shall never die." We cannot believe that he who was so right about so much else could prove wrong in this ultimate matter.

We believe in the triumph of life because of the results this faith produces in those who build on it. Recently a friend of mine received a letter from his friend, which said in part:

Sometime within a year or so I shall be privileged to make the great experiment and discovery of the survival of mind and spirit over physical organism. My gateway to

103

that discovery is one of attrition, but I am grateful to the medical advancement of recent centuries for palliatives and physical help. This personal situation does not leave me perturbed in the least. I suffer no self-pity; the eternal grace is abundant.

For the ensuing year he wasted away with an incurable cancer. During most of that time he placed himself in the hands of doctors doing cancer research and underwent a series of operations that offered no hope of cure, but only multiplied the pain, in order that they might discover whatever they could to ease the way for some other sufferer. That was a thwarting experience at its worst. But it was not frustration! His personal victory was part of the world victory our age most desperately needs. When faith in immortality, lived out in such a gallant passing, gives such victory over death, we cannot believe it false. Only truth sustains the ultimate struggles, and those who live and die by this faith unquestionably are sustained.

II

Beyond the gates of death we expect not only that life will continue, but also that in it personal identity will be maintained, personal purposes worked out, personality still come to full expression. This, basically, is what the Apostles' Creed means when it says, "I believe in . . . the resurrection of the body." Supposing this article of the creed to speak only of the reanimation of the flesh and bones that have been laid in the ground, many men and women of our generation have no little trouble with the creed at this point. That, however, is not at all what Christianity affirms.

This article, rather, is a graphic way of saying that the eternal life in which Christians believe is not, as some men have supposed, the life of a raindrop returning to the sea, in which all personal identity is lost. It is not the immortality of one whose biological heritage has passed on in the loins of the race. It is not the immortality of one who lingers in the memories of those who knew him or in the influence that continues in his wake. It is not the immortality of one who now lives as a thought reabsorbed in the mind of God. None of these things is what Christians mean by the life everlasting; and the creed safeguards the thought of personal identity by the graphic words, "I believe in . . . the resurrection of the body."

In this, Christian thought follows a trail blazed by Paul. Stubborn realist that he was, Paul could not believe in the eternal life as a mere continuance of disembodied spirit. If personality lives, he maintained, it must have some organ through which it can express itself. So, he believed, it must have a body.

What kind of body? This question, he replied, is not too difficult. We see the bodies of grain put in the ground and new bodies come forth. "What you sow," he pointed out, "is not the body which is to be, but a bare kernel. . . . But God gives it a body as he has chosen." (I Cor. 15:37-38.) There are many kinds of bodies, and what is raised is not what was placed in the ground. "So is it with the resurrection of the dead," he continued. (15:42.) "It is sown a physical body, it is raised a spiritual body. If there is a physical body, there is also a spiritual body." (15:44.) Thus the living spirit has its means of life and expression. But Paul

105

was not so naïve as to suppose that the physical body is reanimated; for, said he, "Flesh and blood cannot inherit the kingdom of God, nor does the perishable inherit the imperishable" (15:50). Believing in the resurrection of the body, we do not believe in the resuscitation of the flesh but in the continued identity of the person.

We believe that the personal interests and desires with which we approach death will continue, and that the unfolding life of eternity will carry on from that point. When a little girl asked, "Will I have a doll in heaven?" her wise mother replied, "You will, if you need one." Pointless though it was to discuss with a young child a life in which material things cease to have meaning, it was utterly honest to reply that her need would be met. Personality continues, and its means of expressing itself are sufficient.

More than one soul who, in a crisis of illness, has been out to the gates of death but returned before passing through has told the story of the beauty and wonder of what appeared in that moment. Was it only a dream? Perhaps. But perhaps, also, it may have been a vindication of Jesus' promise to the dying thief on the cross next to his, "Today you will be with me in Paradise" (Luke 23:43). Jesus seems to have believed that life goes on, not after some millennial interruption in the grave, but in instant continuity; for to Martha's declaration of belief in a "resurrection at the last day," he replied with the correction, "I am the resurrection and the life; he who believes in me, though he die, yet shall he live, and whoever lives and believes in me shall never die."

III

After passing through death's door, we expect, finally, not only that life will continue and that personality will go on in unbroken development, but also that this continuation of personal interests and activity is so real that the judgment under which we stand will be incidental to it. Judgment need not be an appearance before the throne of God for sentence to be pronounced. It may equally well be the steady working out of the implications of the things we live by and for; and there is much in the New Testament to indicate that this was Jesus' own view of the matter.

In a book which he presented to the father of Dick Hall, of Dartmouth, after the young man's death, Calvin Coolidge wrote the following inscription: "To Edward K. Hall, in recollection of his son and my son, who have the privilege by the grace of God to be boys through all eternity." So the President pictured the loveliness of a life in which his boy could be spared the hardening of body and mind that often accompanies age. "To be boys through all eternity!"— it is a lovely picture. And yet, there are ominous overtones. Suppose they were to go on in an eternity of perpetual immaturity, of never accepting responsibility, of never growing into interests deep and strong. What drudgery such an eternity could become!

Set over against that, the prayer offered by William R. Harper, former president of the University of Chicago, who as death approached prayed, "May there be for me a life beyond this life; and in that life may there be work to do, tasks to accomplish." Such an eternity, devoted to the pursuit of vital enterprises, given worth-while things to do in a world where strength never runs out, could be heaven indeed.

Jesus seems to have thought of judgment as the outgrowth of things for and by which we live; for as reported in the Fourth Gospel, he said, "This is the judgment, that the light has come into the world, and men loved darkness rather than light, because their deeds were evil" (3:19). So! Judgment not God's sentence, but our choice! Have you ever spent a rainy day shut in with people whose interests all ran so counter to your own as to leave no common ground on which you could stand in any conceivable pastime, no common interest on which you could converse? What a judgment the narrowness on both sides had pronounced upon you!

Or suppose you were suddenly privileged to make a trip to some lovely spot in Europe, of which you had dreamed and read and studied, but which you had never dared to hope you might actually visit. All the stored interests of the years suddenly come to life, and the trip for which you had had no time to make specific preparation would be an endless delight. What a glorious judgment the years of wide-ranging interests would then bring in their wake!

That, said Jesus, is how the judgment is. Think of living eternally in a world of the spirit with a God you have never learned to love! Suppose all your interests have been only worldly, fleshly interests; and now you live in an eternity where these are meaningless. Suppose you have refused the way of love and forgiveness and have learned only to live by avarice and revenge and grudge bearing; and now you have to live with your bitter, isolated self eternally. Suppose, even, that from that other life you might look back and see with a new clarity the evil consequences of the narrow, selfish life you had lived, as they work themselves out in this world. What a judgment that could be!

Or suppose a better thing: that your life has been opened to the love of God, so that to be with him is your joy, to do his bidding is your highest privilege, to live by the standards of his kingdom the aspiration of your life. This, too, is judgment; but its quality is heaven. Would that you and I might learn to live that triumphant life of the spirit!